# THE COMPLETE BOOK OF
# WOODCOCK HUNTING

# BOOKS BY FRANK WOOLNER

THE COMPLETE BOOK OF WOODCOCK HUNTING

MODERN SALTWATER SPORT FISHING

GROUSE HUNTING STRATEGIES

MY NEW ENGLAND

THE COMPLETE BOOK OF STRIPED BASS FISHING
(with Henry Lyman)

THE COMPLETE BOOK OF WEAKFISHING
(with Henry Lyman)

TACKLE TALK
(with Henry Lyman)

THE SPORTSMAN'S COMPANION
(with Henry Lyman, E. C. Janes, and Clyde Ormond)

SPEARHEAD IN THE WEST
(with Maj. Murray H. Fowler)

# THE COMPLETE BOOK OF
# WOODCOCK HUNTING

Frank Woolner

Foreword by
William G. Tapply

THE LYONS PRESS

This book is dedicated to all whose wrists bear honorable scars, whose shirts are wet with perspiration, whose boots collect tickling tidbits of upland chaff: to sportsmen who, with their marvelous gun dogs, haunt birch slopes, popples, aromatic alder edges, and holly thickets where a mystical, entrancing little game bird makes it all worthwhile.

Library of Congress Cataloging-in-Publication Data

Woolner, Frank, 1916–1994.
    The complete book of woodcock hunting / Frank Woolner;
    foreword by William G. Tapply.
        p. cm.
    Originally published: Timberdoodle! New York : Crown
    Publishers, 1974.
    Includes bibliographical references (p. 163).
    ISBN 1-58574-082-9 (pbk.)
        1. Woodcock shooting. 2. Woodcock, American.  I. Woolner,
    Frank, 1916–1994. Timberdoodle! II. Title.

SK325.W7 W66 2000
799.2'4833—dc21

00-038447

Printed in Canada

# CONTENTS

FOREWORD                          vii

INTRODUCTION                      xiii

1  •  Whistledoodle!                 1

2  •  The Singing Ground            25

3  •  Black-Powder Days             33

4  •  Flights and Fancies           43

5  •  Woodcock Cover                53

6  •  The Easy Mark                 75

7  •  The Feather Finders           93

8  •  The Guns of October         109

9  •  Uniform of the Day           125

10 •  Say Grace!                   139

11 •  Tomorrow and Tomorrow       153

     Selected Bibliography        163

     Index                        165

# FOREWORD

When I was much younger than I am now, I asked a grizzled old out-doorsman to tell me all about woodcock. He rubbed his chin and gazed up at the sky. "Well," he said, "they eat worms, and they whistle when they fly, and they migrate. That's about it."

"But," I persisted, "how do you locate them?"

He squinted at me and shrugged. "Woodcock," he said, "are where you find 'em."

I figured the old buzzard was putting me on. But after decades of hunting woodcock, I've come to realize that he was telling me everything there was to know. Woodcock eat worms and migrate and whistle when they fly, and otherwise they are mysterious and elusive and altogether entrancing.

Nobody understood this better than Frank Woolner.

According to the Seneca Indians, after the Maker finished creating all the creatures of the earth, He looked around and realized He had some leftover parts lying around. There was a small pile of feathers—not big flashy ones, for those had been given to the glamorous species He had already created, but drab earth-toned grays and browns. There was a head, but the brain was upside down, and the ears were misplaced in front of the boggled eyes, and the beak was disproportionately long. He found a chunky little body and stubby legs and sturdy but grace-less wings. It was an ill-matched assortment of parts, but because the Maker hated to waste anything, He put them all together and called it a woodcock.

The Maker realized he'd shortchanged the little bird in the body-parts department, so He compensated by giving the woodcock an extra amount of courage, stamina, intelligence, and mystery.

Ornithologists and others who speak Latin call the woodcock *Philohela minor,* which means "little sun lover." It's actually a misnomer. Woodcock travel by night and hunker in dark boggy places by day (although those of us who hunt them are never surprised by where we find them). Observers who saw them poking their long beaks into the ground in search of worms, their main nourishment, called them bog suckers and mud snipe. They've been called Labrador twisters and mud bats because of their erratic flight, and night partridges because of their nocturnal ways.

Their most common nickname is "timberdoodle," which perfectly captures the personality of the little bird. *Doodle* derives from a German word meaning "fool" or "simpleton," hence *doodlebug.* Woodcock, in fact, look like big insects, and they behave like pranksters. *Doodle* also means "divining rod," which conjures up the image of a small bird poking its long beak into the wet earth. Woolner suggested "whistledoodle," an apt nickname that recognizes the distinctive sound of a flushing woodcock, but as far as I know, "whistledoodle" hasn't stuck.

Those of us who have made their acquaintance know the woodcock to be a peculiar, private, funny-looking, and altogether lovable little bird. Aside from serious ornithologists, a few dedicated biologists, and a small but passionate breed of peculiar, private, and lovable sportsmen like Frank Woolner who hunt them in the fall with pointing dogs and double-barreled shotguns, few people have ever even seen a woodcock.

Woolner writes that the woodcock is "a shorebird oddball that has forgotten its ancient origins and prefers thick, moist, brushy uplands to the aboriginal edges of the sea. It is a secret and retiring atom of life, so given to elusive comings and goings in shadowy woodlands and the dark of night that millions of Americans are unaware of its very existence."

This worries those of us who hunt them and love them. Americans everywhere write letters to their legislators and donate large sums of money to conservation groups when the population declines of gaudier, more public birds like eagles and bluebirds are documented. Widely hunted game birds such as quail, ducks, and ruffed grouse have their own well-funded and politically savvy organizations dedicated to their preservation. Woodcock, meanwhile, cling to the coattails of the Ruffed Grouse Society, primarily because they share the same habitat and have historically been a happy by-product of grouse hunting.

*The Complete Book of Woodcock Hunting* covers just about everything anyone would want to know about the American woodcock: how to spy on them during their passionate springtime mating dances, how to select and train dogs that will find them, how to choose a suitable shotgun, how to shoot them (and how to fabricate an effective alibi when you miss), and how to cook them.

But this book omits the most important fact about American woodcock. It's this: For the past twenty-five years—roughly the time that has passed since this book was first published—woodcock numbers have been declining at the steady and terrifying rate of 5 percent per year. The culprit, according to the experts, is loss of habitat.

In part, of course, it's the inexorable spread of civilization, the bulldozing and paving of the landscape that indiscriminately destroys the habitat of all wild creatures. Frank Woolner knew all about this, and he railed against it. "If you're a cynic," he wrote, "the law seems to declare that biological ecosystems must be maintained—*unless* the destroyer files a plan that documents their proportion of destruction and promises to make amends. Having prepared such a blueprint, the developer may then tear the living earth apart, divert its streams, drain its wetlands, fill swamps, and kill all flora and fauna thereon. The paranoid assumption is that nature will not be affected, even though gravel, tarmac, cement, and steel replace peat bogs and alders."

Good woodcock cover is tangly and shadowy and boggy. It's not good for much except harboring woodcock, and since most people wouldn't recognize a woodcock if they saw one, they tend not to value the bird's habitat or see much purpose in preserving it. Twenty-five years ago, the spread of gravel and tarmac and cement and steel appeared to be the main threat to the prosperity of woodcock, and Woolner's tempered optimism made sense.

But the encroachments of civilization turn out to be a relatively minor factor in the loss of woodcock cover. In fact, there are more acres of woodland in New England today than there were one hundred years ago. Far more devastating to woodcock (and grouse and other species) has been the gradual maturing of our northern woodlands. Forest-fire prevention policies, restrictions on logging practices, and well-meaning but misinformed efforts to preserve rather than manage wilderness have combined to produce mature forests with high, thick canopies that prevent sunlight from reaching the ground. The rich mixes of hard and soft woods, bushes, briars, weeds, and vines that blanketed the New England landscape half a century ago are giving way to tall homogeneous forests. Without brushy understory, sun-drenched open patches, and thick tangly edges, woodcock and a myriad of other species are left without shelter, forage, or nesting grounds.

Adaptable species such as ruffed grouse are suffering, but they're hanging in there. Woodcock aren't particularly adaptable. Their needs are quite specific. Earthworms comprise over 90 percent of their diet, and they must have soft, boggy earth under their feet and low cover overhead. They simply cannot thrive in mature forests.

I have no doubt that had Frank Woolner known of these developments, he would have written a different book. This one is cheerful, quirky, optimistic, opinionated and anecdotal, full of stories and debates about men and dogs, hits and misses, guns and recipes. "Nothing," wrote Woolner in 1974, "—not the clearing of lands, the guns of sportsmen, or the killing pesticides—has entered [the woodcock] on the lists of endangered species. He is prospering, still trading up and down the old flyways in spring and fall."

Alas, today the woodcock is not prospering. In this respect, you can read *The Complete Book of Woodcock Hunting* as a memoir of a happier, simpler era. Seasons and bag limits have been steadily reduced for both the Atlantic and the Mississippi flyways, but biologists agree with Woolner that men with guns are the least of the woodcock's problems.

Frank Woolner was a serious—albeit self-taught—natural historian and a passionate sportsman, and his love affair with woodcock glimmers in every word of this important book, which has been out of print for too long. He was born in 1916, lived his entire life in central Massachusetts, and died in 1994. He considered himself a political independent and a religious agnostic. Those of us who knew him can vouch for his straight-shooting Yankee independence. Read his words about woodcock and you'll understand that he was, in his way, a highly religious man. His cathedral was the out-of-doors, and his pulpit was his writing desk.

When Frank Woolner came home from the Second World War in 1945, he became a full-time outdoor writer. He had no college education, so he learned his craft by reading and writing and rewriting, and before he was done, he'd published hundreds of articles and several books on hunting and fishing and nature. He wrote a weekly outdoors column for his local newspaper, and for 32 years he reigned as editor-in-chief of *Salt Water Sportsman*.

Although Frank Woolner's name is most closely associated with surf fishing, he was, like many sporting writers of his era, a generalist. He wrote as knowledgeably about wildflowers and tree frogs as he did about woodcock hunting and striped bass fishing, and he came by his knowledge firsthand. If you didn't find him at his typewriter, you knew he was outdoors, taking whatever the season offered. He fished for every species that swam in fresh and salt water, and he hunted every bird and animal that was legal. When nothing was in season, he tromped the fields and woods, looking, sniffing, listening, and learning. When he wrote about it, you knew he'd been there.

It would be a mistake to regard *The Complete Book of Woodcock Hunting* as just another how-to hunting book. Woolner doesn't even begin to discuss hunting until chapter six, and of its eleven chapters, only four are devoted to hunting and shooting. In "Black-Powder Days," he gives us the best history I've read anywhere of the market-hunting era. "Say Grace!" contains tried-and-true woodcock recipes from hunters and their wives (including my mother). The balance of the book is natural history, a well-considered mixture of Woolner's own observations and those of fellow hunters and game biologists and other writers.

He devotes an entire chapter to the charming courtship ritual of the woodcock. I have reread it dozens of times, and I always get a tingle. It's simply as good as outdoor writing gets. Listen: "Never have I been close enough, or had hearing acute enough, to catch the soft, gurgling note that biologists say precedes the peent, but I watch my springtime friend strut back and forth, beak down and very proud of himself. His movements are vaguely reminiscent of the shorebird clans: he bobs when he walks, like a flesh-and-blood toy. He buzzes at intervals. Suddenly he flushes, flying low and fast for 50 or 60 feet before spiraling upward. Up, up—to a dizzying height, where my glasses catch him again, hanging on fluttering wings some 200 to 300 feet above the somber, winter-killed earth, etched against the deepening blue gray zenith and the white sparks of stars. At flush, even my old ears have caught the wild twitter of wings, a sound that every upland gunner of eastern America will carry to his grave as a touch of paradise previewed."

*The Complete Book of Woodcock Hunting* is an informative and entertaining book—certainly among the best ever written about the American woodcock. But more than anything else, it's a love letter from an incurable romantic to the elusive object of his passion. "It is unthinkable," Woolner concludes, "to contemplate a world bereft of woodcock. We need comings and goings in the cold springtime and the hectic flush of fall. I still envision timberdoodles etched against a full moon, even though I know that this is ridiculous—but is there any man of our company who wars against a dream? Love timberdoodle, but never take him for granted. Count him an easy mark at your peril. Protect him forever."

    Amen.

—William G. Tapply
Pepperell, Massachusetts

# INTRODUCTION

Now it is early October and a full moon is rising over trees heavy with foliage. The air is warm and a few late-summer insects still shrill their death songs, waiting for the scythe of hard frost. From the rising ground of my backyard in central Massachusetts I can see white birches and alders, a slope of brambles, the edges of dank little swamps, and forgotten apple trees fighting their way out of fox-grape tangles and juniper. Woodcock are there, but I only sense them: they are invisible in this luminous night.

Standing in the twilight, swatting an occasional late mosquito and peering into the dusk, I am fully aware that neighbors would consider me strange if I admitted to worshipping at the shrine of a curious little game bird, a blithe spirit of the woods, a happy poltergeist, a soft brown creature of immeasurable beauty and deep mystery.

Men who study woodcock and men who hunt them all fall under the same spell. In our minds, moonlight and woodcock go together. Whether this is so or not, those of us who delight in this shorebird that deserted the sea eons ago are profoundly stirred when the moon is full in October. We imagine soft wings in a silver twilight, and hordes of migrants dropping into favored coverts. If there is a touch of frost at dawn, so much the better—they *must* be flighting!

And so we go afield in the crisp, jeweled mornings of early fall, well bundled against chill, and then perspire as the sun mounts and summer fights its delaying action against ultimately triumphant autumn. There will be heavy foliage and spider webs and dogs, fractious after a long summer of inactivity.

If all of the Red Gods smile, there will also be woodcock. They'll come twittering out of cover and swiftly disappear into that tropical jungle while we wait for a clean shot and feel the perspiration burn our red-rimmed eyes. It will be better later, after the first hard frosts. Perhaps, on a few golden mornings and bracing afternoons, it will be perfect. We deal with an un-predictable quarry.

The American woodcock (*Philohela minor*) is unique. Though very plentiful within its considerable range, few—other than ornithologists and upland-shooting enthusiasts—have ever seen or would be able to identify the bird. Our grand little longbeak is a refugee from the seashore and dwells in the woods; it flies by night and rests in secluded thickets during the day. There one may find the "chalk" of droppings, and there—when red maples flame and the world is gloriously fevered by autumn—shooting enthusiasts and pointing dogs savor a touch of paradise.

In the proper season there are native birds in all coverts, from the cold Maritimes across to Manitoba's southern hinterlands, through Michigan and Minnesota, then down to the rich parishes of Louisiana. True, gunners usual-ly account for migrants trickling down ancient flyways or arriving en masse. Classicists, observing old usages, speak of "a fall of 'cock," rather than the American "flight." It doesn't matter; semantics cannot alter facts. The birds come and go, triggered by some infallible physiological time clock we mortals have yet to explain.

A few great admirers, grim of visage, think it degrading to call a wood-cock a timberdoodle. I disagree. This is a name bestowed by America's pioneers, and it is no less objectionable than "night partridge" and "Labrador twister," each of which evokes a pleasant image. Although "big-eye," "mud snipe," and "bog sucker" may be questionably evocative (and you are at lib-erty to accept or reject my own "whistledoodle"), colloquial names add a full measure of romance.

Some excellent books have been written about woodcock; hopefully I do not presume too much in attempting a personal update. Certainly it is doubtful whether anyone has ever attained wealth by scribbling about, or painting pictures of, this strange little ghost of the gloaming. Great outdoor writers and illustrators of the past simply became lyrical when they chronicled Burt Spiller's "little russet feller." The paintings and etchings of Alexander Pope, A. Lassell Ripley, and Lynn Bogue Hunt were inspired by something far more than an artist's God-granted skill. The magic is there, ensuring a measure of immortality for these creative men whose fond memories enabled them to go beyond perfection.

Game biologists, too often members of a cold and calculating tribe, are similarly impressed. A steady procession of great research technicians have been overturning the stones of ignorance. Almost always, such pro-fessionals spend more time with the ecology than they do with the romance and skills of hunting. This is right and proper, for the knowledge amassed by savants keeps us on a solid foundation. Such selfless men often find their most astonishing discoveries relegated to the files of other researchers; such men are too rarely published in the popular magazines, and their books too often are buried in the libraries of the scientific community.

I have learned much from the findings of these men, and will quote them. If you desire the sum total of information to date about our weird little longbeak, then you must delve into a whole host of sophisticated papers. Some books and articles are out of print, and others are not easy to obtain. Many of the publications are too technical for public consumption, yet a few bridge the communications gap.

I am impressed by *The Ecology and Management of the American Woodcock* by Howard L. Mendall and Clarence M. Aldous. This was a publication of the Maine Cooperative Wildlife Research Unit at Orono, Maine, in 1943—and I doubt that copies are readily available. The work was a classic in its time and is still carefully studied by game-management students. Many feel that Mendall and Aldous cannot be topped.

William G. "Bill" Sheldon, of the University of Massachusetts at Amherst and formerly of the United States Fish & Wildlife Service, is the current authority. He has put it all down, giving full credit to predecessors and adding much of his own research in *The Book of the American Woodcock*, published by the University of Massachusetts Press in 1967. Dr. Sheldon is an upland hunter and a bird-dog fancier, so it was perhaps inevitable that he would spend much of his adult life studying the most mysterious and retiring of our game birds. His work is currently accepted as gospel by students and by gunners desiring the latest in biological findings. It is, in short, practically all that mankind knows about *Philohela minor* at this time, though Bill Sheldon would be the first to say that further study is indicated. Studious types must have this volume. I certainly recommend it.

Dr. Leslie Glasgow of Louisiana has been a leader in the business of woodcock research. For many years it was said that he had banded more timberdoodles than any other person or group of people in the nation. He may still hold this honor, although recent years have witnessed much banding in northern states. Glasgow, like Mendall, Aldous, and Sheldon, is a titan: he has contributed more information about wintering woodcock than any other man in our time.

By the nature of things, there are romantics—and book men. Call me a reporter. I plan to mix a brew of factual information about the bird and its life cycle, hunting strategies, dogs, guns—and the romance that hairy-chested outdoorsmen deny even while they are mesmerized by a setter's bulging eyes on point, the hipper-dipper flight of a tawny target, and the absolutely wonderful feeling of rapport with nature in a clean, aromatic arena. Those of us who enjoy a short harvest—a couple of months in the fall—and then case our guns, to spend the rest of the year admiring a grand quarry and insisting that it be protected, will understand.

Shooting is climatic, yet it comprises a very small segment of each wheeling year. No upland gunner is less enthusiastic about spring arrivals than about fall migrations. Who, other than a lover of woodcock, would be willing to stand in the chill twilights of muddy, soul-sickening March to welcome incomers? Who else can shiver so deliciously with a combination of raw cold and the spine-chilling recognition of a miraculous homecoming?

Then, too swiftly for those of us who have attained middle age, it is October again! Now we greet with a lover's ecstasy the wild, tortured hillsides where brambles tear a man's wrists, and the alder runs where hunting boots are never quite adequate to prevent a knee-deep plunge into a hidden seep. There is frustrating foliage, green for the most part and only clotted with the scarlet of red maples. Shirt-sleeve weather–and spider webs, and birch aphids that tickle. It is always too hot and the cover is too thick, and the panting dogs are eager to plunge into every woodland pool. But it's Opening Day!

Armed with open-bored shotguns loaded with Number 9 shot (or even 10s where some strategist seeks an edge), we all thrill to the twittering flush of a woodcock kicked out of sere fern and underbrush ahead of a dog that has become a statue in the shadow and shine of low cover.

And we miss! Lord, *how* we miss those early birds!

Often they are slow off the launching pad, fluttering skyward with all of the orientation of a bewildered night moth awakened at high noon; but they have a grand ally in screening foliage. No sportsman wants to reduce a precious game bird to tattered remnants at short range, so the conscientious citizen waits through agonizing ages of time—actually shaved seconds—and then the target is utterly lost in a sea of shimmering green leaves.

Gradually, frost and fall winds clear all decks for action, and there are a few paradisiacal days when the trickle-through migration is healthy, or, occasionally, when some unusual combination of weather conditions up north precipitates a true flight. Birds grow warier and more aerobatically adept as the season progresses.

Woodcock are unpredictable. Up to a certain point you can figure grouse and pheasant and quail, because all are resident. Timberdoodles come and go in the hours of dawn and dusk. Chalk doesn't mean they are there—only that they *have* been there. Moreover, the migration is relatively swift—encompassing no more than six weeks or a couple of months at best in transit areas, although stragglers afford spotty shooting before and after the great phalanxes pass through.

In any event, one has a sense of wonder—of something transient and beautiful, perhaps unreal. A woodcock is occult, a living spirit of the land we have inherited and have never quite succeeded in conquering or domesticating. Every timberdoodle is a reminder that the American wilderness endures and prospers in spite of urban sprawl.

We hunt a bird that is not a very difficult target, but one that cannot be second-guessed. Maybe it will be there, and maybe it will not. If the birch hillsides and the mixtures of alder runs and popples are well inhabited, then it may tower at flush—or perhaps go out low and fast like a jinking snipe. If a woodcock is slow, then he is aerobatically agile. Just about the time you get on and press a trigger, he is likely to change direction or sideslip. Any whistledoodle is quite capable of making a fine wing shot look like a bumbling amateur.

Obviously, I am fond of woodcock. There is even a slight possibility that I delude myself in placing the ruffed grouse on a higher pedestal. The grouse cannot be excelled as a game bird at a specific moment in time and space, but neither can the timberdoodle. It is all a matter of timing.

My woodcock is quite as wild as any grouse, no spawn of the effete game farms. He is an easier target (usually) than the canny partridge, but he stirs my imagination because he is a spirit of the gloaming and the unknown. I have collected him in numbers and have relished his flesh as a gourmet meal. He has humbled me on many occasions.

Therefore, so long as I can tramp the woodlands in health and with reasonable safety, I will respect the "little russet feller" whistling through white birches or alders or popples. He will destroy me when the foliage is thick and when I am keyed to the faster flight of a grouse, and he will shoot me down in flames when I get fatuous and consider him an easy mark.

I am not superstitious (aside from an aversion to driving green automobiles) and I do not believe in miracles. Hence, we must protect this delightful little game bird and guarantee its well-being in a world of "progress" that destroys coverts and spreads poisonous insecticides that kill as many organisms as they protect.

Finally, bowing to learned studies that show no effect of moonlight on our weird little friend, in either migrating or feeding, I am wistfully hopeful that those of us who love a superb game bird will be allowed a few hopeless delusions. How can it hurt to believe, like witch doctors of some aboriginal tribe, that woodcock flight on a full moon?

I dote on a full moon in October and November, and I know that I am wrong. I don't care: my dreams have always been full of timberdoodles towering over alders and white birches, and I see those wiry branches etched against an earth-satellite that our astronauts have proved to be just another hunk of dusty real estate. Must stainless-steel technology destroy romance?

Since it has done so after a fashion, we'd better progress to cold fact. Sorrowfully I do so, but triumphantly I note that our wizards have yet to explain some very interesting phenomena.

How does a woodcock navigate unerringly from Louisiana to the covert of its hatching in southern Canada? How does the adult bird know precisely when to move southward or northward? How do traveling timberdoodles zero in on ground where earthworms have been plentiful for years on end? Why does a pointing dog unfailingly locate a live longbeak, yet often appear nauseated by the scent of a dead bird?

We know the way of a snake on a rock, and we think we know the way of a man with a maid. Do we know the secrets of the wild creatures?

I have no ready answers. If you can offer solutions, I forgive you. Otherwise, we are all men who grope for truth, mean well, and hope that woodcock will always fly in cold moonlight, in dawn and dusk, over the points of staunch old dogs when it is time to harvest a precious natural resource.

# WHISTLEDOODLE!                    1

## Life-style of a Poltergeist

Lacking familiarity with or empirical knowledge of woodcock, any reasonably intelligent citizen may be excused for raising an eyebrow when told of a shorebird that has deserted the sea, flies by night, and boasts a long, prehensile bill and an upside-down brain. Add to this description the fact that its ears are located ahead of its eyes and you have an odd specimen indeed.

All of these things are true of *Philohela minor*, the American woodcock. There is just one member of the clan in the New World, although a larger cousin entrances European sportsmen. Rarely, through some fluke of nature, one of these big and beautiful foreigners—*Scolopax rusticola*—is observed on this side of the Atlantic. Supposedly accurate birdmen have reported single specimens at such widely divergent points in the United States as Virginia, Pennsylvania, New Jersey, and Rhode Island. Rare sightings have been recorded in Canada's Province of Quebec and in Newfoundland.

I mention this at the outset because no cracker-barrel session ever omits some tale about the flushing of a European woodcock in a North American covert. It *can* happen, although such an occurrence is far less likely than being struck by lightning.

We deal exclusively with *Philohela minor*, order *Limicolae*, family *Scolopacidae*—a shorebird oddball that has forgotten its ancient origins and prefers thick, moist, brushy uplands to the aboriginal edges of the sea. It is a secret and retiring atom of life, so given to elusive comings and goings in shadowy woodlands and the dark of night that millions of Americans are unaware of its very existence. That's a big statement in view of the fact that woodcock are very plentiful through southern Canada and the entire eastern half of the United States.

If the woodcock did not exist, then some science-fiction writer might well have to describe it as a bird from some far planet. Chunky and short-coupled, a timberdoodle's neck seems to be part of its shoulders. The bill is long, and its tip is prehensile in order to probe for and seize earthworms. The lower third of this amazing appendage is equipped with delicate nerve endings to sense the location of prey and guide its capture. There are protuberances on the underside of the upper bill that act almost as teeth, and the long tongue is rough surfaced. Nostrils are set very high to facilitate breathing while the bird is probing.

The eyes of a 'doodle are large, set well back and high on the head. Some say this enables the bird to see aft while probing forward. Others feel that, since the huge luminous eyes are particularly adapted to darkness, woodcock have a measure of myopia in daylight flight and a corresponding tendency to flush toward any bright opening in screening foliage. Perhaps. But some of the small males, and even the chunkier females, will on second flush go twittering away through a latticework of interlocking twigs and branches; they don't seem to be bothered by any deficiency of vision.

Curiously, *Philohela*'s ears are positioned ahead of its eyes, between the base of the bill and the eye sockets, something rarely found in bird or beast. There is a good possibility that, in addition to sensory nerve endings in the bill, hearing is also brought into play in that never-ending search for worms below the ground's surface. Perhaps scent is a factor too in this search.

A feeding woodcock often thrusts its bill into moist earth and then pauses as though gauging vibrations. A moment later it will move quickly, a few inches to right or left, and probe again—this time zeroing in on an earthworm. Various grubs are avidly consumed, but worms are most important, and a healthy longbeak may consume more than its own weight in squirmers during a given twenty-four-hour period.

Physiologically, the woodcock is a shorebird, heavy-breasted to ensure stamina in flight. Its heart is a great pump, surprisingly large in so small a package of life. All 'doodles have inverted brain cases. Thanks to specialized adaptation, unique in birds, the cerebellum has been forced back and down so that it is actually upside down, providing space for the great high-set eyes and the ears. No other bird in the world is so conformed.

An adult hen woodcock will average 7.3 ounces in weight, whereas the male typically weighs about 5.8 ounces. A female's bill usually measures

Woodcock on nest. *Photo by Jack Swedberg, Massachusetts Division of Fisheries and Game*

2¾ inches or slightly larger, though her mate's will be under 2½ inches. Length of the three outer wing primaries has been called 99 percent accurate in establishing sex: a female's outer primaries will measure more than 12.4 mm; the cock's will be less than that.

Evolution has provided natural camouflage for most of the world's wild creatures, and never has the art been more thoroughly consummated than in the case of the woodcock. A mature 'doodle not only blends into the rich brown and gold of ground cover, but also seems to become part of that royal mosaic. In the hand, this bird offers an overall impression of russet, but there is much more to its color than that. Shoulders, wings, and rump are subtly barred and blended in shades of dark brown, gray, and sunny glints of dull gold. Beyond a high and sloping gray forehead, the crown is dark, almost black, cross-marked with slim bands of gold. A woodcock's breast and underwings are beige, each of the soft breast feathers being dark at the base and shading toward the color of well-creamed coffee at the coverlet tips.

A ridiculous little wedge-shaped tail is a medley of brick-red and black feathers until—in strutting—that appendage is raised and spread; then it is graced by an edging, light gray above and pure white underneath. A timberdoodle usually assumes the display attitude when wing tipped, brought down and facing a grim executioner.

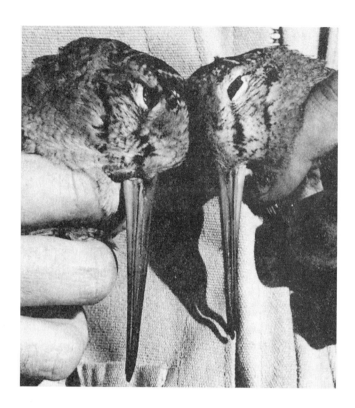

Bill length is one indication of sex. Female, left, boasts a considerably longer bill than the male at right.

Sheldon notes little difference in basic coloration between cock and hen, but I think that the former is invariably darker. The subject is always good for an argument. John Alden Knight, for example, cited prevailing thought and then told how he and a friend sexed nine birds by color alone. (Is there a possibility that choice might also have been influenced by size?)

Generations of sportsmen have wrongly assumed that small 'doodles are "flight," and larger ones native. Sexing is tricky—easy for scientists but difficult for the everyday gunner. For all practical purposes, it is logical to assume that a large bird is a hen and the little guy a cock rooster. This applies at any season; woodcock lose little weight in migrating.

Because *Philohela minor* is migratory, the species is controlled by international agreement. Seasonal shooting frameworks and bag limits are decreed by United States and Canadian government agencies whose game biologists carefully monitor populations and attempt to prevent overexploitation of a valuable renewable resource. Overshooting, before the turn of this century, threatened the very existence of woodcock; now, elimination of summer gunning, together with reasonable fall shooting seasons and meager bag limits, has restored the beige beauty. As a matter of fact, timberdoodles are underharvested on Southern wintering grounds.

Whistledoodle's range is almost precisely half a continent, extending westward in southern Canada from the Maritime Provinces to Manitoba—

then down through all of the states from eastern Minnesota to New England and southward to the Gulf of Mexico. A majority of birds breed in the north and winter in the Deep South, chiefly in Louisiana, but also in the Carolinas, Georgia, Alabama, northern Florida, and Mississippi. Louisiana is a major wintering ground and the focus of heavy migration from Canadian provinces and states lying west of the Appalachian Mountain chain. Tremendous numbers of birds flutter southward with the first chill blasts of a northern winter and return in the spring. It should be noted, however, that a minority remain south of the Mason-Dixon line as true residents, and others peel off to raise broods in each state along the north-south flight path.

Northern boundaries of prime breeding grounds stretch across southern Canada from eastern Manitoba through New Brunswick, Nova Scotia, and Prince Edward Island. Northward, though thinning, birds summer in southern Newfoundland.

In the United States this massive brooding territory extends from Maine to central Minnesota, then southward through New York, New Jersey, and Pennsylvania. Usually, the farther north you go within this region, the

Dr. William G. Sheldon, one of America's foremost game biologists, prepares a mist net to trap migrating woodcock in the spring. *Photo by the Hampshire Gazette*

6

Gardner M. Hobart and Bill Sheldon examine and band a woodcock caught in a mist net. *Photo by the Hampshire Gazette*

greater the concentration of birds. New Brunswick may well be the "woodcock
capital of the world."

During a hunting season the gunner often feels that a timberdoodle
is mute, its only contribution to sound being a wild and unearthly twittering
at flush. This piping trill is caused by the passage of air through a woodcock's rapidly beating primaries; it is typical, yet far from a solo performance.
Most of the bird's notes are reserved for use on spring singing grounds or
in the annual raising of a family.

There is, first, the "peent"—a metallic buzz reminiscent of a cicada in
August. The sound is insectlike, hardly something you'd expect from a

game bird. It is a nasal challenge, thin, yet loud in the cold silence of an early spring twilight. It is a sound like the chain saw of an elf attacking the dry shards of a dead summer's underbrush.

On the singing grounds (discussed in Chapter 2), dominant male woodcock establish territory and initiate regular dawn and dusk flights to advertise their virility and command of the ground. Flush usually is accompanied by that wild twitter of air keening through primaries, and the season prompts other language.

Spiraling down after a triumphant flight, woodcock make a new and different liquid trill, called by some the "kissing sound." It is musical and aboriginally beautiful, absolutely right against a background of dusk and red west and the first glinting of stars in a blue gray zenith.

If a hen appears, drawn to this aerobat of the twilight zone, yearning for some unknown union which burns within her immaculate printed circuit of blood and brain, then one may also hear a soft gurgling note, usually uttered by the male but sometimes by the female as well. This has been variously described, by Sheldon as "tuko," by others as "turkle," or just as a melodious gurgle. The sound is low pitched, so one must be close to hear it. Almost always the tuko precedes the peent, but is used singly as a cock bird approaches a hen.

A male woodcock defends his singing ground against other males, and he is a mighty feisty little cuss at this time of year. An interloper is chased out of darkening skies in dogfights that recall the old days on an almost forgotten western front. The combatants chatter rapidly, sounding a brittle clackety-clack that—if you are an incurable romantic—might be compared to the ancient machine guns of Spad and Fokker, or the cackle of a miniature pheasant.

Later, brooding a clutch of immatures, the hen utters a variety of sounds, each apparently a command to wayward chicks. These include a soft nasal chatter to call chicks that have scattered and a warning squeal—almost feline—a rapid *cac-cac-cac* to indicate danger. There is another sharp squeal, often accompanying the broken-wing routine used by several game birds to lure predators away from nest or young. There is a low-key whicker to indicate slight alarm, a hawklike whistle, albeit much less audible, and a high-pitched "whee" uttered by chicks in distress. All of these have been noted by such excellent authorities as Sheldon and Pollack. I have heard some of them, but not all.

The male woodcock is no great shakes as a husband. In fact, he's a rakish old stay-out-all-night who takes his damsels where he finds them, and then deserts home and hearth while the hen raises a brood. The singing ground is his domain and he calls successive ladies to court. They come winging in over the budding hardwoods and alders, little beige beauties entranced by the magic of creation and the siren song of a chevalier in

Typical nest and four-egg clutch of woodcock.

springtime's annual reincarnation of Camelot.

A male will mount successive females and travel from one singing ground to another at the height of a season. For almost two months he will perform at dawn and dusk. Singing continues in the north on a diminishing scale through June and has been reported in July. Actually, the exhibition has been witnessed during each month of the year, but is climactic in early spring.

Male woodcock take no interest in the building of a nest, the brooding of eggs, or the education of fluffy chicks. When the procreative urge subsides, whistledoodle père becomes a loner, a flitting shadow in the night, and a solitary old man of dank thickets. No male woodcock recognizes his children.

The hen is family minded. She nests early, building a shallow, cuplike depression on dry, brushy ground. Many such nests will be close to a singing ground, but rarely within its confines. There is no evident camouflage aside from surrounding brush, because the hen's coloration is enough. Nests may be found in abandoned overgrown fields, in a variety of warm, brushy areas, and in mixed growth of birch, aspen, and conifer. Usually, nests will be within one hundred yards of a singing ground, and are seldom easy to locate without the aid of a fine pointing dog.

There is little research to support the idea, yet it seems reasonable to suppose that an unusually wet spring may flood out a percentage of home-sites. In this case, and also where early clutches are destroyed by predators, there may be a second attempt at nest building. Usually, and this is normal, the American timberdoodle brings off no more than a single brood each year. If there is a second, then more than three eggs would be a rarity.

Like so many shorebirds, the woodcock produces an astonishingly large egg, roughly the size of that deposited by a ruffed grouse, and one wonders how so small a flyer manages. Usually there are four (occasionally five), colored faint pink to cinnamon and blotched with darker spots. Although there are the usual tragedies laid to predation, the success ratio is astronomical compared to that of many other birds. Woodcock bring off a high percentage of each brood.

An incubating hen is loath to leave the nest, even when man or animal intrudes. She broods those precious eggs for twenty-one days, covering them when the sun is high and leaving her treasure to feed during warm night hours. There may be a reason for this behavior that has so far escaped savants. I am convinced that birds do not brood eggs simply to keep them warm or cool; they do so to shield the incubating embryos from deadly radiation, which is directed earthward by the sun and builds to excessive levels during peaks of sunspot solar flare activity. Ultraviolet is a known killer of simple cells; hence, it is astonishing to find that few scientists have investigated the brooding of birds as a possible shielding device.

Hal Lyman and I in 1973 presented a rough hypothesis about this phenomenon as it possibly affects year classes of striped bass. We found that a fair-to-massive bass hatch usually coincided with minimum sun-flare activity. It may well be the reason why trout and salmon bury their eggs in gravel—not to prevent dispersion by currents but to shield them from radiation.

In presenting this hypothesis, we opened a Pandora's box of possibilities. Later we learned that game biologists and ornithologists have found remarkable correlations between sunspot activity and the cyclic fluctuations of lemmings, varying hares, cottontail rabbits, and other imperfectly described cyclic species. In addition, researchers had noted that the sunspot cycle affects migration in certain birds. It is only fair to add that this early research was marred by some perplexing contradictions. Nobody seems to have investigated the effects of radiation on the eggs of birds.

Having studied the striped bass, it was a short step for me to suspect that many birds, even in areas where temperatures are ideal during periods of incubation, shield their eggs from radiation produced by a usually beneficent sun. I would remind scoffers that the woodcock is famous for bringing off most of its brood successfully—and the woodcock is a tight brooder. Hens, unless disturbed, remain on the nest all day, and feed at night. Is shielding one secret of success? We need some bright young research technicians who are not crippled by the usual blind acceptance of existing data and who are willing to investigate.

The woodcock hen broods for twenty-one days, and then there is an imperious stirring within each egg. A longitudinal slit appears in each of these imperfect spheres—again, something very unusual—and the chick struggles out, wet and bedraggled. It's an ungainly thing, with Cyrano's nose and shockingly big feet.

Like so many game birds, the woodcock chick is precocious; within a few scant hours it is dry, fluffy, and agile enough to travel. There is no long period of immaturity in a nest. The chicks are immediately up and off, following the hen into a green and gold world. Two days after hatching, the entire brood may be one hundred or more yards from a natal site, busily foraging.

Woodcock travel almost continuously, rarely over any great distance but often crossing country roads where motorists report "some strange new bird with a flock of chicks." To my suburban office, one morning in mid-May, there came an excited mail carrier. "You won't believe what I saw!" he exclaimed. "A crazy-looking brown bird with a long beak and four chicks hardly bigger than thimbles. What can they be?"

Without further discussion we repaired to the site. (The postman parked his blue-and-white truck in my drive, thus further slowing the already irregular delivery of the United States Mail, and we used my Chevy.) After all, a bird so strange in appearance that it might have arrived in a UFO is

Broken eggs: a nest that has been destroyed by predators.

worth investigating. But I thought I knew what it was.

"Right here," he said presently. "They all crossed the road and they were in no hurry—I had to tramp on the brakes. Seems to me there were four little ones, kind of fluffy and gray brown. They went into those brambles."

By this time, I knew, the hen and chicks could be well into concealing cover, but we parked and I advised caution. It is always easy to step on a longbeak sprout, for they are marvelously camouflaged and often freeze at the first hint of alien sound. This time the old girl was easy to locate: she was crouched, curiously enough, in a little gravel island between some grasses, not a yard off the blacktop. I was towering over her, with my moccasined feet close, but she remained immobile—a beautiful bird, glittering eyes wide open, apparently frozen in suspended animation.

Wordlessly, I beckoned my postman. He came tiptoeing in, gazed solemnly, and declared, "I never saw anything like that in my life. Hadn't we better report it to the Audubon Society?"

As we backed out, I tried to convince him but doubt that I succeeded. He'd lived in New England for forty-odd years, yet the timberdoodle was unknown to him. Little green men from Mars would have been no less exciting. Such curious critters as timberdoodles do not exist in the minds of average citizens.

Lacking a staunch pointing dog, I sought no chicks. They'd be somewhere in that tangle of dead grass and brambles and leaf mold, pressed against the ground, waiting for the hen's reassurance. A random search would have been futile, and we might well have tramped on one of the chicks. It was far better to leave them alone and return to gainful labor, strangely elated. A hunter, in springtime, is this world's most fanatic of puritans; it was enough to know that the old magic of creation was working.

Hen woodcock are good mothers, absolutely fearless, and depart from their broods only when there is no alternative. As a result, it is often possible to capture them with a wide-mouthed net, and is easy to locate them with the aid of a pointing dog. When a hen flushes, as she will as a last resort, she'll launch into the air with legs dangling and tail tilted down. Like the ruffed grouse, a female timberdoodle is likely to use the old broken-wing trick, luring a predator away from immature chicks and then bursting into free flight at the last possible moment.

Game biologists and hunters since the beginning of recorded time have declared that a woodcock—either the European or the American variety—will carry its young on an escape flight. Some say that the chick is gripped between the hen's thighs, others that it rides on the mother's back. I have never seen this, and modern authorities are skeptical of it. Sheldon says he never saw it, and wonders whether the tail-down flying attitude of a hen with chicks may not have fostered an illusion. No photographs of passenger-

Tail-down flight attitude of a hen woodcock flushed off her nest.
Some biologists feel that this accounts for reports of hens carrying
their young aloft.

carrying 'doodles have been taken, yet the belief goes back to antiquity. There is no indisputable proof one way or the other.

Immediately out of the egg, woodcock chicks are tiny, agile fluffs of life. Their bills are impressive even then, measuring 15 mm, and will lengthen rapidly—so regularly that a trained biologist can age them precisely. The bill of each chick grows at a rate of 2 mm per day; therefore, one simply adds a day of life for each couple of millimeters of bill length. The feet of the freshly hatched tiny 'doodle are almost adult-sized, so banders use the same ring diameters on both chicks and mature birds.

These grotesque little characters are ideally camouflaged and terribly difficult to find, even though, through the offices of an accomplished pointing dog, you know they are there. Like a grouse chick, the miniature timberdoodle will flatten itself against leaf mold and brushy undergrowth to lie motionless and almost invisible. It would be easy to step on one and, unfortunately, a good many well-meaning naturalists have done so.

These babes of the woods are so perfectly dressed that one can easily confuse them with the dead leaves and grassy debris of ground cover. As one searches diligently, sure that nothing is there, the chick suddenly materializes like a bit of ghostly protoplasm. It is rather shocking to make this discovery, for the living creature is nothing more than a pattern overlaying a similar pattern. Unaccountably, it is there! A thing that the eye has scanned and missed, suddenly and mysteriously glimmers up into human consciousness. No man ever finds a woodcock chick without marveling at the miracle of natural camouflage.

The chicks are best left alone. On the nest a hen is strangely docile. She will even occasionally submit to being touched by the human hand. She will flush only when that seems to be a last resort. Uncontrolled dogs can be bad news, and it is certain that house cats and roving domestic mutts wreak havoc on young broods. There is only one good reason to seek out the young, and that is the professional desire of a wildlife technician to capture, band, and release immatures. Even in this case a dog should be tied after the initial point, and the search for chicks should be conducted very carefully. It is a game for experts.

Woodcock chicks grow very rapidly. Marshaled by a hen, the brood patters through springtime's warm wonderland. Almost always there are four fledglings, each maturing at an astonishing pace. The little longbeaks will be probing for worms and other invertebrates two days after they have emerged from their eggs. In less than four weeks they'll be almost full grown and flying like their parents. Six to eight weeks after hatching, individuals go their separate ways, becoming loners in the bush. Now, only the immortal printed circuits in their strange, upside-down brains will guide them in feasting through a summer—and then flighting southward to the bottomlands of a benign Gulf Coast. There is magic in it, or at least there is

Chicks are so beautifully camouflaged that they are hard to find.

Having located chicks, a pointer is tied down. Bill Pollack and
Dick Woodard band fledglings.

Fledglings nestle in a hat after biologists have collected them.

something strange and wonderful that we humans cannot understand.

Timberdoodles largely subsist on earthworms, yet they also take other invertebrates and a spice of tender vegetation. One is forced to wonder what the northward-migrating woodcock finds in a cold land upon first arriving during any wintry springtime. Often the ground is frozen and snowdrifts streak ancient singing grounds. There are seeps along brook beds, and a few worms may be found there. Open streams may also provide a minimum fare of snails and other protein.

Earthworms comprise 90 percent of all food ingested, but the 'doodle will accept a variety of insect larvae, ants, moths (occasionally caught on the wing), tender ferns, and some seeds. Snails are readily consumed and may be an important diet item when migrants first arrive in the frozen north.

Moist feeding grounds are a necessity; hence, a dry season will concentrate 'doodles wherever there are seeps. The adult bird may ingest more than its weight in earthworms during every twenty-four-hour period; most feeding, however, is confined to the early hours of nighttime and to the pre-dawn period. Adults drink a surprising amount of water and, curiously, do not tilt their heads back to drink in the manner of most birds—a timberdoodle sticks his bill into the water and sucks up a cooling draught.

Dick Woodard and Bill Pollack carefully band the fledglings.

Where worms are concentrated in moist thickets, whistledoodles often feed in daylight, but banquet tables are most lavishly spread in the dim light of dusk and dawn. Immediately after sunset, each velvet-winged flyer zigzags out of protective loafing cover and repairs to relatively open fields where hunting is good. This is common practice among wintering migrant woodcock in the Deep South. Even in the North, where brush and moist soil often assure worms, a dry summer will see dawn and dusk journeys to well-watered open areas, even to suburban lawns, where humans are startled by their batlike arrivals and departures.

Bill Pollack, chief game biologist of the Massachusetts Division of Fisheries and Game, has advised me that there is another reason for timberdoodles' dusk and dawn flight—the fledglings are exercising breast muscles. This seems logical, and is further proof of the danger of declaring that any supposedly normal woodcock activity can be explained simply.

Our funny little game bird is peculiarly adapted to digest worms. Its throat passage terminates in a very elementary stomach that can hardly be called a gizzard. Below this there are many intricately coiled intestines—the so-called "trail" that so many Europeans relish and so many Americans cast

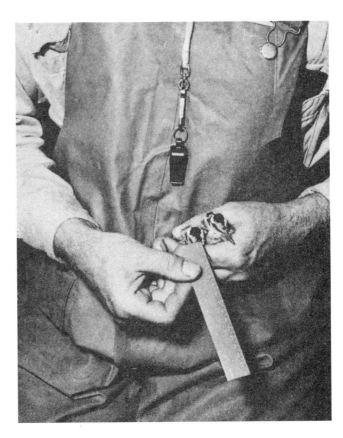

Bill Pollack measures the bills of fledglings. Length provides a highly accurate assessment of age, almost to the hour.

aside. Digestion is exceptionally rapid, accounting for that amazing food ingestion of full body weight during a twenty-four-hour period. The breast of a woodcock is dark, all rich muscle, to ensure sustained flight; the drumsticks are light flesh. Gourmets savor both.

By early summer at the latest, woodcock broods are broken up by mutual consent, and each little longbeak becomes an individual adventurer. Where concentrations of them are flushed by curious humans, the availability of earthworms—rather than any sociable convention—is the key. There is a time of hidden molting in dense thickets during late August. There are solitary comings and goings in the soft light of dawn and dusk, but there is little straying from natal territory until early fall when some slant of sunlight jogs a subconscious printed circuit.

Then there is a strange unease gnawing at the vitals of each russet flyer, an awareness that is no part of knowledge or experience, yet is an irresistible urge to follow the sun and seek a southward trail blazed only by genes and mores unknown to the bird and quite as poorly explained by ornithologists. The exodus begins earlier than is generally thought and builds to a peak with the first hard frosts and snowfall of a northern autumn.

Guided by forces that we cannot understand, woodcock come fluttering

# WOODCOCK SEX AND AGE CRITERIA

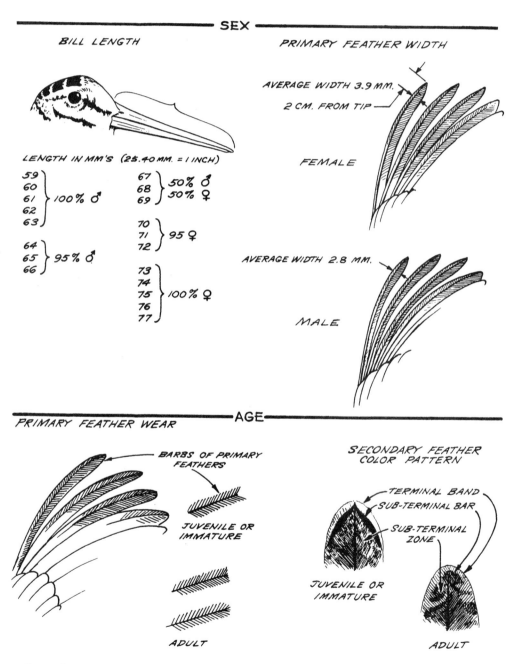

**SEX**

BILL LENGTH

PRIMARY FEATHER WIDTH

LENGTH IN MM'S (25.40 MM. = 1 INCH)

59
60
61 } 100% ♂
62
63

64
65 } 95% ♂
66

67
68 } 50% ♂
69   50% ♀

70
71 } 95% ♀
72

73
74
75 } 100% ♀
76
77

AVERAGE WIDTH 3.9 MM.
2 CM. FROM TIP

FEMALE

AVERAGE WIDTH 2.8 MM.

MALE

**AGE**

PRIMARY FEATHER WEAR

BARBS OF PRIMARY FEATHERS

JUVENILE OR IMMATURE

ADULT

SECONDARY FEATHER COLOR PATTERN

TERMINAL BAND
SUB-TERMINAL BAR
SUB-TERMINAL ZONE

JUVENILE OR IMMATURE

ADULT

Sex and age criteria prepared by Steve Liscinsky, Pennsylvania Game Commission.

down the two or three principal flyways, braving the guns of October, foul winds, man-made obstacles, and that deadliest of all enemies—hard cold. There is murderous attrition, yet a surprising percentage of migrants conquer all enemies to arrive at their final winter feeding grounds by mid-December or early January. Louisiana boasts the greatest concentrations of woodcock then, although all southeastern states host a fair share of travelers.

Some of this vast number are taken by hunters during the southland's winter shooting season, yet few Dixie gunners have ever been so entranced with woodcock as have their blood brothers in the North. Southerners usually prefer quail, and bobwhites take much pressure off timberdoodles. There is a modern flush of interest in the longbeak as a sporting bird on southern grounds, but nothing compared to the fever of the North. Fortunately, the gun is a minor factor in woodcock mortality. There are other hazards, including natural predators, but the primary cause of attrition is the advance of civilization.

Happily, the woodcock, in spite of its silky appearance and apparent vulnerability, is a very tough little cookie—able to survive wounds that would send another bird to Valhalla. Those which are wing tipped by guns often recuperate and fly south long after the man-made armistice. More are caught by sudden onslaughts of frigid weather and freeze to death. A sudden heavy snowfall, if winds are foul and there is no way to flutter southward, can be disastrous. Cold and subsequent starvation is a major killer.

Then there are the hazards created by mankind. Woodcock annually break their necks colliding with power lines, lighthouses, and tall buildings. They often make fatal contact with speeding motorcars, a destiny shared by practically every species of wild game residing in mechanized advanced nations. There is no help for it, since it is unlikely that the clock can be turned back.

Mankind harasses whistledoodles in other ways. There is, of course, the "development" that denudes a former singing ground, and there is fire. Drainage projects remove feeding grounds, but are no immediate threat if adjacent areas are available. Unfortunately, the developers of this nation seem to harbor a lust for low, moist ground—it seems a challenge to buy cheap, fill, and then produce a burgeoning empire of chain stores and apartment buildings.

Woodcock, like all wild creatures—and like man—are beset by disease and a multitude of parasites. These result in a measure of mortality, but nothing too dire or spectacular. Natural ills have been with us since Creation, and most of them have been contained. These ills are irritating, yet are seldom responsible for any massive kills. So far, game biologists have isolated a number of woodcock parasites and diseases, but none appear to be important as mass killers.

Pesticides pose an important threat to woodcock. Earthworms accumu-

H. G. "Tap" Tapply and Brittany spaniel, Bucky, with early-October birds in central New Hampshire. *Photo by Pal Alexander*

late vast reservoirs of the stuff without suffering any ill, but they pass on this poison to birds.

There is adequate documentation of timberdoodle kills traced to insecticides, usually heptachlor, in the Gulf states. DDT is cited as a major threat to woodcock in the North, yet almost no deaths are recorded, and there is no evidence of human illness caused by the ingestion of woodcock liberally laced with this agent. Nobody knows whether there may be progressive declines in the health of bird or man through accumulating increasingly great bodily reservoirs of chlorinated hydrocarbons or similar chemicals.

New Brunswick, in 1970 and partly in 1971, supposedly pushed a panic button. They closed woodcock hunting seasons because scientists examining birds found a high level of DDT in fatty tissues. Laboratory technicians were undoubtedly right in their analysis, yet there seems to be no evidence of corresponding illness in timberdoodles or man. In fact, though woodcock are absorbing discernible increases of chlorinated hydrocarbons, their population appears to be increasing rapidly. No human being has died, or even become ill, from eating this bird's flesh.

Can we relax?

Certainly not, because mankind still speculates on a cutoff point where the accumulated poisons may work their ills, at which time it might be impossible to beat a retreat. Earthworms are supposedly resistant, but what if residues finally reach a point fatal to them? Many birds would be deprived of natural food and would die. Man would suddenly find no natural aerator of the living earth; that simple little catastrophe is horrendous to contemplate.

Fortunately, there is now public denunciation of pesticides capable of killing an entire ecosystem while supposedly controlling a few pests. Rachel Carson sounded a tocsin with her inspired *Silent Spring*, and the Tartar hordes of despoilers have been checked. It is worth a double take to note that Carson *never* advocated an end to all pesticides; she simply demanded that they be used reasonably. She has been abused by idiots and misquoted by fools, but Carson's voice will never be silenced. That frail little woman was a giant.

Hopefully, guided by her genius and by our own common sense, we will do better. Perhaps we will even restore a good part of the life-giving biological ecosystem. We'd better, else hunter and do-gooder alike had best kiss the living world good-bye.

For woodcock, there remain natural predators, including humankind. Incubating 'doodles often abandon a clutch of eggs when frightened off the nest during the first days of brooding. Domestic dogs are great destroyers. House cats may be the deadliest enemies of all. Skunks delight in a woodcock omelet, as do opossums, raccoons, and black snakes. Any owl capable of catching a timberdoodle is a menace. Shrikes are fully capable of taking immatures, and do so. Cooper's hawks and goshawks hit adult and immature alike. Crows are great nest robbers and have been known to attack stuffed woodcock used as decoys. Squirrels have a taste for their flesh in the spring. Foxes, both red and gray, challenge their normal survival. The list of natural foes is considerable.

Nonetheless, a majority of well-informed game biologists and sportsmen now feel that natural predation rarely exerts any undue mortality upon woodcock. The great killers are weather conditions and the steady encroachment of mankind's desecration of a wet and viable woodland. In this arena, natural enemies and the guns of autumn are inconsequential.

Woodcock, if residence can be established by their annual time on a site, are northern birds that spend a few pleasant winter months Down South. They follow the sun. They leapfrog up and down the continent, flying by night and resting in broad daylight. Their time of arrival in many areas is entirely predictable, in spite of inclement weather. Whistledoodle meets his commitments.

# THE SINGING GROUND    2

## A Field of Romance

No northern springtime would be complete without the return of woodcock. Just thinking about it, I feel a shiver of anticipation, and a fear of pneumonia.

Here in central Massachusetts the advance guard arrives in mid-March, and it is pretty punctual. I can practically guarantee a trim, zigzag flyer on the fifteenth, though they may come earlier or later. In 1972 a close friend of mine spotted one parachuting into some alders protecting a frigid brook bed on March third. One year later a considerable number of birds passed through on the tenth.

In Yankee country, by the third month of the year a man is thoroughly sick of winter and is searching for any hint of the vernal equinox that seems lost and forgotten. There'll be a steady procession of red-winged blackbirds and grackles by mid-March, and I then expect to see a bluebird, feathers ruffled by chill east winds. Since renewal of life is as solidly based on faith as on proof, it is high adventure to keep a rendezvous in a suburban clearing.

I go there well bundled against the cold, boots crunching through the dirty snow that melts by day and crystallizes at night. There is no sound other than the groan of trucks on a distant highway and the mournful sigh of a bitter breeze sieving bare hardwoods. Nothing is reminiscent of springtime, not even the color of the sunset: it will be all venomous green and lemon—

a promise of more cold and piercing wind. No matter, I have a blind date with a poltergeist.

Phlegmatically buttoning the goose-down jacket around my throat and adjusting my binoculars with clumsy, gloved hands, I wait in the sparse shadows of a skeletonized birch. The lowering sun gutters in an icy curdle of cloud formations. Every tree branch stands out, wiry and brittle against the glowing west. There is no movement: all the world seems locked in an elemental freeze. Knowing better, I still feel that this is a fool's errand. In spite of warm clothing, the chill of March seeps through; it is hard to maintain a vigil when every nerve screams for a dram of good scotch in front of a blazing fire.

Of course, there are fringe benefits: human beings rarely understand the rewards of quiet observation, yet this is the only way to enter the world of wild creatures. While waiting for woodcock, I have seen a red fox pounce on a mouse; once a great horned owl swung low over my clearing, so close that I could almost feel the slipstream from his soft primaries. There are always a few ducks and geese trading back and forth at this season during the witching hours, hurtling silhouettes against a flaming sunset—further proof that winter is taking a long count.

The woodcock mating display usually begins at a moment almost precisely that of the transition between daylight and darkness. It is too late for available-light photography and too early for the strobe-etched close-up. Stars are just becoming apparent as tiny diamond points of light in the soot blue zenith. It is the quiet hour, still and cold. Always my teeth are beginning to chatter when the first miraculous visitor arrives. Strange how that sight warms my blood!

Sheldon and other biologists have concluded that evening flights are most likely to begin when the light has diminished to a reading of 5.0 to .02 footcandles, but Sheldon notes that behavior varies with individual birds and the location of singing grounds. If a male timberdoodle's daylight resting or feeding territory is adjacent to a chosen field, he may walk in rather than fly.

Like an Indian, I trust no light meters or other instruments other than my eyes and awareness. Scientists must be completely accurate; hence, they lose a share of aboriginal wonder. It is much nicer to expect company immediately after a star becomes visible, when the sun has plunged over a jagged, black western horizon and its light reflects only on some high-flying commercial jet plane sighing over the top of the world.

My 'doodles usually appear well above stricken hardwoods, far up in the vault—just familiar shapes on direct passages. Frantically, I center the jiggling binoculars and watch a bird drill overhead, circle, make a second and perhaps a third pass before pitching into a scruffy patch of alders and broken weed at the far end of my clearing.

Touchdown! The play begins and I know the script: it has been per-

Early-season safari, walking into cover with setter.

formed throughout my life year after year—and for a million years before—yet always it is new and exciting. If I am lucky, the light-gathering lens will pick him up, often forlornly perched on a snowdrift under the blackened brambles and dead goldenrod of a spent year.

All discomfort is forgotten and my imagination races. This astonishing, mystic little bird has arrived weeks before the ground will be fully unlocked. What will he eat? Will he live on the fat accumulated in a winter of foraging the rich bottomlands of our Gulf Coast? He must have expended much energy in a long flight northward, but he's home free and thinking of romance instead of sustenance.

I am cursed with poor hearing. My father grew deaf in old age, and I will follow him down that pathway—so now I must cup an ear and curse the odd truck grunting up an incline on the state highway five thousand yards away. It is imperative that I hear, as well as see, him peent! It is as much a part of springtime as the first scent of a skunk cabbage broken in the hand, the first thin piping of hylas in an awakening land. I *must* hear it, and I do!

He bobs forward, indistinct yet still sharp in the field of my binoculars. It almost seems that this sound is produced by hard physical effort. It is a metallic buzz, insectlike, much like the abrasive note of a cicada in August, but much shorter in duration. I needn't have worried about my failing ears, for the peent is loud in a March twilight.

Never have I been close enough, or had hearing acute enough, to catch the soft, gurgling note that biologists say precedes the peent, but I watch my springtime friend strut back and forth, beak down and very proud of himself. His movements are vaguely reminiscent of the shorebird clans: he bobs when he walks, like a flesh-and-blood toy. He buzzes at intervals.

Suddenly he flushes, flying low and fast for fifty or sixty feet before spiraling upward. Up, up—to a dizzying height where my glasses catch him again, hanging on fluttering wings some two hundred to three hundred feet above the somber, winter-killed earth, etched against the deepening blue gray zenith and the white sparks of stars. At flush, even my old ears have caught the wild twitter of wings, a sound that every upland gunner of eastern America will carry to his grave as a touch of paradise previewed.

The twittering continues, muted by distance, and then he is zigzagging back down, sometimes darting from side to side, occasionally falling like an autumn leaf, and again settling like a parachutist. The song has changed; now it is very different, not the shrill piping of wind through stiff primaries. My bird is really singing, uttering the liquid "kissing note" through its prehensile bill. It is a ventriloquial sound, difficult to locate, coming from everywhere and nowhere.

If the light endures, I may applaud successive performances over a period ranging from half an hour to forty-five minutes—even more, if the moon is full. Sometimes, as though to confound the experts, there will be sporadic encores well after deep night has cloaked the landscape.

Depending upon human hearing acuity, one may trace all of that remarkable performance by sound alone. I can't do it, but others can. I remember an afternoon on the West Branch of the Penobscot River in Maine—a late afternoon, for four of us had returned to camp and were broiling squaretail trout over an open fire when a woodcock began his singing flight at the far end of a little clearing hacked out by a lost generation of loggers adjacent to the Falls of Debsconeag.

It was late May and the black flies and no-see-ums were bothersome. We'd admired, but had not desecrated, a little patch of yellow violets. All of it was pure magic—four men living rough and feeling fit and catching herds of trout and salmon, most of which we released. The woodcock, like the cow moose that lumbered through our clearing one morning, was lagniappe.

This timberdoodle was singing earlier than usual, well before sunset. We heard him peent and then flush. Intrigued, we made a stalk and witnessed successive performances. Each time he vaulted into a slowly darkening sky, Arnold Laine would profess to hear that wild and musical twittering throughout, even at the apex. "Can't you hear it!" he'd exclaim.

Johnny Clark, cupping an ear, agreed solemnly. "Like the bells of Saint Mary's," he said reverently. Charley Whitney and I, attuned to the peent and the flush and the kissing song close to earth, were scornful of our companions who claimed to discern a melody at three hundred feet, over the rush and chuckle of a turbulent river. I'm sure we were wrong.

It's different when there are no background distractions, no brawling stream or traffic profaning the twilight silence. Out in wild country, silence is almost oppressive and the least sound is magnified. An Indian, or a well-attuned white hunter, sifts out each subtle click and scratch and thin song of the wilderness; each tells a tale as surely as sight does.

A singing ground—or call it a singing field—is a clearing. Well, not really a clearing, for it usually features low brush. There may be stunted clumps of alders and birches, highbush blueberries, junipers, and low conifers. There is sure to be a rimming of trees, always stark against a dramatic sunset at this time of year, and birds seem to come from some indeterminate point well beyond it. In most cases they arrive shortly after sunset and may remain through the night, though singing is ordinarily confined to short periods at dawn and dusk.

The clearing may be large or small, and some appear more attractive than others, serving successive generations of woodcock until the brush grows up and the land matures. Sheldon and his fellow researchers have noted that timberdoodles need a certain amount of "runway area" for takeoffs and landings, so the small field is most often surrounded by low trees, and larger clearings may be bordered by woodland giants.

Food is of minor importance here. Some singing grounds offer earthworms—after the ground softens—but more are barren of sustenance. Strategic placement is most important, because woodcock usually nest anywhere from a few feet to several hundreds of yards from a trysting location.

In hilly country a singing ground may be located on a slope, yet landing spots invariably are flat, brushy benches. They can be far back in wild land, or in the suburbs close to well-traveled highways and human habitation. Only one thing seems certain: if a ground is ideally positioned, it will be occupied year after year—until such time as saplings grow into trees, or "progress," in the form of housing or industrial development, utterly destroys a natural habitat.

Woodcock, like so many other migratory birds, apparently return to the area of their birth. Therefore, adult males are more likely than transients to take command of clearings that they know dimly from preceding years. Transients search for untenanted grounds and are quick to take possession of any territory that, for one reason or another, is temporarily abandoned. Often there are bitter little battles, but almost no evidence of casualties.

Males come first to establish a territory. Their metallic peenting, twittering flush, and kissing song serve twin purposes: to establish a territory and warn off other males, and to attract little, soft brown ladies. Both endeavors succeed. Interlopers are chased away and plump females come swinging in.

The peent and the gurgle are sexual manifestations, but a woodcock harassing another male that has invaded its singing ground clatters furiously. The two twist through the darkening skies, and the pursuer sounds a rapid cac-cac-cac note that sounds like the ripping of taut canvas. Occasionally, combatants collide in midair and fall to the ground on soft wings, yet there is no documented evidence of injury resulting. As is usual with birds, advantage accrues to the possessor of a territory. Many animals enjoy the same advantage; even a domestic dog establishes a home territory, and much larger dogs will skirt that ground because occupancy ensures rights.

It has been amply demonstrated that a singing woodcock performs in a relatively short period of luminosity at dusk and dawn—resting, feeding, or remaining dormant during the dark hours. Yet when a guttering full moon hangs over a spring landscape, this romantic play is extended well beyond the usual cutoff point. Light appears to be very important.

There may be exceptions. Tap Tapply and I correspond like junior-grade pen pals. We discuss everything from the first red-breasted nuthatch of a winter season to the yarding of deer and the state of a grouse's "snowshoes." One late March he told me that he had heard a woodcock singing at 11:00 P.M. on the periphery of his New Hampshire digs, and I went immediately to the calendar. There had been a half-moon—not full, but still a source of illumination. Did we have something unusual, or very normal? I don't know. It was certainly unusual to have Tap awake at such an hour, because he usually hits the sack at 9:00 P.M. and is up at dawn.

A. I. "Pal" Alexander with early-season birds taken in New Brunswick, Canada. *Photo by Pal Alexander*

One thing is certain: woodcock sing at dusk and dawn, extending flight time when the moon is brilliant, and then melt into the surrounding landscape, often flying several hundred yards from the field of romance. Dawn's singing may actually encompass a greater length of time than that of dusk—at least this is the conclusion of game biologists.

You are unlikely to find timberdoodles in any clearing after the spring sun has blasted out of an eastern horizon. They are creatures of the half-light—strange, big-eyed gnomes. Count on a woodcock to arrive shortly after sunset—if the arena suits his taste and if it is adequate. Count on him to be there again at dawn.

Nor do I know what constitutes "adequate." Perhaps it is simply a relatively open space in a sea of high canopy, but there are fields and openings that never host a bird. Consider it a place that is partially open and partially clothed with low brush. When you find such a spot and verify its appeal through observation, then the "little russet feller" will return as regularly as the swallows are said to visit Capistrano.

Every singing ground is a place of romance, and little more. Males take possession, and their acrobatic, melodious flight both warns off other males and attracts hens. Mating takes place there, although nesting may be anywhere from yards to more than a half mile from the nuptial site. Rarely is any nest built within the confines of a true singing ground: this is a place for hanky-panky, not for the rearing of families.

It is also a place for the first encounter annually for northern sportsmen who hunger for a first glimpse of the bird they adore. Nothing quite so thoroughly destroys the fiction that winter is unconquerable than a timber-doodle flighting in from a semitropical coast in March.

Then one can forget the raw east wind, the snow in the black growth, the cold, and the chill, lemon yellow sunset. Woodcock on a singing ground prove that spring is here.

# BLACK-POWDER DAYS     3

### Shooting, Away Back When

It is surprising to learn that woodcock hunting in America is a comparatively new sport, evidently dating back only to the early 1800s. Prior to that time, first settlers apparently ignored a game bird that must have been abundant. Although they may be excused for seeking larger game—such as deer, wild turkeys, grouse, waterfowl, and hares—it is rather astonishing that Englishmen in a new world would ignore a smaller look-alike of the much-prized European woodcock.

That they did so is evidenced by an almost complete lack of mention in their literature, and is bolstered by the first known reference to *Philohela minor* in 1634. At that time a man named Paul Le Jeune was reported to have said, "Woodcock were eaten by the Montagnois tribe of Iroquois in the vicinity of Quebec City."

Without doubt, American Indians throughout woodcock range were fond of timberdoodles, and they probably employed one hunting tactic later adopted by white pioneers—firelighting. It has been said that an Indian will eat anything that does not eat him first, but nobody can fault the red man's taste when it comes to a plump woodcock.

Certainly there was a measure of shooting by the late 1700s, a time when spaniels were used to flush birds—and when local boys, armed with sticks, were employed as beaters. Gunners, armed with heavy muzzle-loaders, advised beginners to wait until the bird had cleared cover and was leveling off. That's still pretty good advice.

Henry William Herbert, an English remittance man who became America's foremost outdoor writer in the mid-1800s under the nom de plume of Frank Forester, added considerable information. Unfortunately, Forester made some regrettable errors—in one of his books a striped bass is drawn with an extra set of fins—but he was respected in those days and his reports must have seemed accurate to a majority of sportsmen. If there was a mite of exaggeration, it is excusable; hunters have always yarned after action. Certainly Forester's accounts must have been near the mark, and he boasted of shooting 125 birds in a day, while possibly losing 40 or 50 cripples!

Moreover, he says that on that occasion he started late in the day and quit shooting at 4:00 P.M. The guns were muzzle-loaders, yet he wrote: "If we had been provided with a fresh brace of dogs at noon, with clean guns, and a proper supply of powder and copper caps, both of which gave out, it would have been perfectly easy on that day to have bagged from 100 to 150 couple of woodcock."

The inference is—two men, each shooting 100 to 150 individual woodcock, or 200 to 300 in all! That would take some doing today, even with modern shotguns and smokeless shells. The old black-powder pieces threw an appalling amount of smoke. Then, and now, it is virtually impossible to see whether a direct hit has been made at the moment of consummation. I have used muzzle-loaders on the skeet field and have always had to ask a bystander whether a clay was powdered or lost.

Forester's slaughter was accomplished on the so-called "drowned lands" of Orange County, New York, in 1839. Fourteen years later, when he published this account, the author declared that 'doodles had become scarce, an observation borne out by other reporters—and not very astonishing, in view of the attrition.

Capt. Adam H. Bogardus, called the "world's champion wing shot," and a surprisingly accurate man with firearms and factual information, said in his book *Field, Cover, and Trap Shooting*, the final, updated edition of which was published in 1891, "The most I have ever killed in one day was fifteen couples. I have heard men boast of having killed fifty couple in a day; but if they did it, the birds must have been vastly more abundant than I ever saw them anywhere."

This 1891 book was a third edition, and Bogardus was then sixty years old. He had earned a reputation as a great hunter and a superb marksman. His stuff, with minor nit-picking, rings true today—and he must have been ranging the American uplands for at least forty years prior to 1891.

No doubt, there were lots of birds and, in the eastern United States, the clearing of land must have helped to increase woodcock populations. Spring, summer, and fall gunning, however, took its toll, and by the early 1850s everyone noted a decline in the number of woodcock. This was the beginning of a heyday in sport shooting and market gunning; both peaked between the end of the Civil War and the early 1900s, when conservationists began to demand safeguards in the form of shortened seasons, smaller bag limits, and an end to kill-for-cash.

It is said that in 1874 market hunters realized $1.50 per couple for birds. This seems excessive, but it's in the records. Remember that inflation had not assailed our nation at that time, and a dollar was a lot of money. It seems incredible that anyone other than affluent gourmets would pay $1.50 for a brace of birds that weighed something less than a pound combined. If it happened, then woodcock must have been placed on a pedestal with hummingbirds' tongues.

My own early research, including interviews with a few of the old market hunters who operated in the late 1800s and the first years of this century, indicates that woodcock weren't much sought after. They were sold along with the money crop—grouse—and, until restrictive laws made black marketing profitable, even the heavier-fleshed partridges brought no more than fifty cents to $1.50 a brace. Some of the old market hunters wouldn't waste powder on a timberdoodle, and those in the Deep South castigated their dogs for pointing a woodcock instead of a quail. It is likely that nobody made much money with whistledoodles.

In the beginning, there was firelighting. It is a very effective technique, and it may still be used by a small minority of poachers who aren't making money but who love to challenge law enforcement officers and eat woodcock. Originally, blazing pine knots were used, a practice undoubtedly originated by the Indians. Later there were oil-soaked rags and then the kerosene lantern. All worked well.

Bogardus doesn't offer firsthand information, but he wrote of firelighting. "I was told that in the South the Negroes go out by night in boats with torches and, paddling along, the woodcock on the muddy margins are knocked down with sticks."

Bogardus *must* have known that white folk as well as blacks employed firelighting. Perhaps he never did it, but others worked the gimmick right up until market hunting was outlawed. They went from the pine torch to blazing, oil-soaked rags to kerosene-, carbide-, and battery-powered lights. Firelighting is a deadly method because the timberdoodle is immobilized by light at night. The same trick was long used by waterfowl hunters to approach and kill resting rafts of ducks and geese.

While Southern Negroes and Indians may have used sticks to bat down befuddled woodcock, white hunters went to open-bored shotguns and fine shot. They gunned the same locations—stream edges and cultivated fields where the birds probed for earthworms at night. Usually the quarry was groundhogged; that is, shot on the ground when its eyes reflected the light of a torch. Some were killed in the air at extremely close range. In the beginning, this slaughter was considered true sport and was a seasonal business.

"Dusking," or "skylining," was another effective technique, very popular with market hunters in the late 1800s. Basically, dusking consisted of pass shooting at birds outlined against the sky as they moved out of daylight resting areas and flew to feeding grounds during the last light of sunset. Those who knew where and how to position themselves often enjoyed very fast action in a swift thirty minutes of sunset's afterglow. Today, of course, there is an armistice declared at sunset, so dusking is practiced only by a few spur-of-the-moment violators who blunder into a massive evening flight and can't resist temptation.

One major problem with dusking was the inability to locate birds brought to earth. Old-timers killed surprising numbers of 'doodles at this time, but they admitted to losing many that were lightly wounded or never located by the dogs. Even in black-powder days there were gunners who scorned sky-lining.

It is easy to criticize, but remember that our grandfathers honestly saw no end of nature's bounty. Many market hunters became ardent conservationists after they became convinced that continued slaughter was a major sin. Actually, tides began to turn in the late 1800s when various states legislated against summer gunning. Prior to that time the unofficial season opened in July. It wasn't the glorious Fourth, as so often reported, although in later years that date became traditional.

The old-timers killed woodcock at all seasons and, where the market was solid, late June was every bit as good as July. By that time immature birds were almost full sized and, though gunners sweated in hot jungle growth while they battled mosquitoes, native 'doodles were decimated long before flight woodcock ranged down the flyways in September and October. The best thing that ever happened to *Philohela* was the Migratory Bird Act of 1918. Thereafter, timberdoodles could be harvested only in the fall. Market hunting was about finished, and the longbeak became more plentiful over its entire range.

But give Frank Forester credit. As early as 1848, in his book *Field Sports in the United States*, he railed against summer shooting. "Enact that the Woodcock shall not be slain—shall not be possessed . . . on plate or in stomach, until the first day of October."

True sport shooting probably began in the mid-1700s, but was not really popular until one hundred years later. There just wasn't any reason to waste powder and shot on a bird that weighed less than half a pound! Stylish gunners got interested in sport shooting immediately after the Civil War, at which time there was a boom period for it. The lads were still using muzzle-loaders, although the new breechloaders were coming in. It was a time of professional market hunting, yet few were very seriously engaged in the business.

In the first place, unless you raised dogs capable of flushing and retrieving, were skillful enough to center a lot of birds, and were able to quit other gainful employment for three or four months during the fall, it was a losing game. None of the great hunters made a lot of money, but they had a lot of fun. All were opportunists; they hunted deer, grouse, woodcock, quail—whatever was in demand. A few were renegades, more were decent citizens; some hunted only for the family larder.

There are some curious old beliefs. Our great-grandfathers called the woodcock a "bog sucker." They thought that the bird never ate anything solid, but drew its nourishment from the soil—sucking up liquid from boggy ground. Don't fault the old-timers—in their time the hypothesis seemed credible.

The first American woodcock hunters used spaniels. These were cockers and springers, the best of an Old World introduced to the New. These dogs worked close, flushed, and were adept in retrieving. Gradually, during the 1800s, sportsmen became intrigued by the pointing breeds and there was more interest in English setters and pointers. In the beginning there was a mixture of long-haired setters, the often nasty-natured Gordon, the Irish, and the true English. Early Gordons were fine, close-working dogs, but some would take your arm off at the elbow if you weren't a bosom buddy. Pointers soon earned a full share of plaudits.

Then, as now, upland gunners experimented with different combinations of bloodlines. Bogardus was sold on a setter–pointer cross, the so-called "dropper," but had good words for the Scottish border collie, a dog "of amazing sagacity." Although the world's champion wing shot favored the pointing breeds, he stated, "The first dogs I shot over were cocking spaniels, and I do not believe they had any breaking at all." The implication was that cockers were natural hunters and required no extensive yard training or field work under a gun.

By today's standards, dogs of the 1880s were big and slow. They performed close to the guns and would have been castigated for "going big." Experienced shooters wanted bloodlines denoting field capability rather than blue ribbons for physical beauty, and they broke their feather finders on wild birds. Miles L. Johnson, a famed Mercer County, New Jersey, handler in the 1870s and thereafter, may have been the first to launch an argument that still flares between field trial buffs and hunters. Johnson wrote, "I assert that whatever the strain of the dog may be, no matter how many prizes at shows his parents may have taken, and how high his price may have been when he was a puppy, he can only be properly broken over game. Nothing else will do, *and nine out of ten of the dogs vaunted about by the fanciers and dealers are practically worthless in the field.*" (The italics are mine.) The statement is intriguing if for no other reason than that it was made more than one hundred years ago, and its thrust continues to precipitate wild arguments among hunters, bench show enthusiasts, and field trial people.

When Forester and a companion "could have shot" 200 to 300 birds a day on the old "drowned lands," muzzle-loaders were in vogue. The fact that the two of them actually accounted for as many as 125 woodcock apiece (plus 40 or 50 cripples lost), in 1839, is rather astonishing. I am not going to engage in calculation, but it should be easy to figure the time element in loading those old black-powder shooting sticks. Timberdoodles had to be present in astronomical numbers.

Somewhat later, as Bogardus reported, bags of thirty woodcock per man were not unusual. George Peabody, a Massachusetts market gunner, logged precisely 220 during the season of 1867. Predictably, with summer and fall gunning, timberdoodle populations declined rapidly. By 1880, Peabody turned to sniping woodchucks with a rifle "because there were almost no woodcock." (By his market-hunting standards, of course.)

Breechloaders arrived immediately after the Civil War, and were the arms that have come to epitomize a golden age of upland hunting. Practically all of the best were side-by-sides, though singles were still used. For that matter, right up until the dawn of this century, some stubborn old coots preferred the muzzle-loader. If it was good enough for father, it was good enough for them! Evolution is a slow process.

The guns were heavy; it is a testimonial to the stamina of these old sharpies that they could carry a bulky hunk of ordnance all day and still come up with bags of game that seem enormous by today's standards. Certainly woodcock were more abundant, but there is no reason to believe that they were easier to rack down in thick foliage. There is no explanation other than a grudging admission that early nimrods were tougher and fitter then we, and they were superb shots.

Bogardus, even in 1891, scorned light smoothbores. He wrote, "A gun of ten gauge, thirty-two-inch barrels, ten pounds, is one for all sorts of uses. It will stop anything that flies or runs on this side of the Rocky Mountains, if properly charged and aimed. Many think ten pounds too heavy to carry, but the advantage of a good solid gun in delivery of fire is very great. I do not like light guns, neither is a cheap arm at all economical."

Later, possibly having second thoughts, he qualified this by declaring, "Some think a gun of ten pounds is too heavy to carry through a long day and use in all sorts of ground. For many a lighter gun would be better for woodcock shooting, and for grouse and quail in tall corn. But I would not recommend anyone to get a gun of less weight than seven and a half pounds for general shooting and good service."

Bogardus was shoveling sand against a high-course tide, and he must have realized it before his last hunt. Still, weighty ordnance continued to dominate through the remainder of a somnolent final quarter century and well into the 1900s. Market hunters used 10- and 12-gauge doubles, often belling the muzzles to achieve a greater spread of shot at close range. Nobody favored the dainty 16, and a 20 gauge would have been unthinkable. These came later, the 16 to enjoy a short heyday before it was almost phased out by today's 20. Twelve gauge has remained the most popular over the wheeling years.

Tradition dies hard, so the side-by-side is still considered classic in upland hunting. Sportsmen treasure fine doubles, and this is healthy since we no longer shoot for record bags. Pumps and autoloaders are more efficient. This is no personal opinion. We have only to study the arms used by market hunters during a strident kill-for-cash era at the turn of the century.

Almost en masse, these old buccaneers retired beloved side-by-sides when Winchester offered a revolutionary Model 1897 pump. The so-called "cornsheller" killed more game, more efficiently, and with greater speed—hence it became the premier tool. Although market hunting was legislated out of existence after the turn of the century, and was almost a memory prior to World War I, the Roaring Twenties offered a lucrative market for illegal waterfowl. Then doubles were used only to finish off cripples. The primary smokestick had become John Browning's autoloader—often featuring an extended magazine tube that would hold as many as eleven shells.

Granted, these professionals wanted the "killingest" shotguns available. They weren't interested in sport per se, and would have used cannons if there was any way to tote the things. As a matter of fact, old punt guns on waterfowl *were* cannons, and it may surprise a few to learn that such formidable weapons are still legally employed off the coasts of Great Britain.

Early repeaters were far from featherweight. One of the first was Winchester's Model 1887 lever-action repeater, a smoothbore spin-off of the "Yellow Boy" that finally won the West after it had settled Custer's hash at Little Big Horn. Strangely, I find no account of the Model 1887's acceptance by market hunters. It was a bulky, six-shot twelve-gauge and the one in my possession—purchased by a late uncle when he was a young man—is no great testimonial to the gunsmith's art. Like so many arms used by upland hunting enthusiasts of that time, this piece has had its barrel cropped to straight cylinder.

The next attempt was Winchester's Model 1893, an improvement that evolved into the famous Model 1897. *This* cornsheller was a natural pointer and a highly efficient hunk of ordnance. When it appeared, doubles were sorrowfully laid aside and market hunters felt that they had the ultimate weapon. Still, the '97 was far from being goose down—it pulled the scales to more than eight pounds.

Winchester persevered and created the superb Model 12 hammerless pump—in my opinion the finest slide-action shotgun ever invented. All Model 12's were heavy by today's field standards, and they are still too heavy, other than in minigauges, for effective work on woodcock.

None of the true upland market hunters ever had occasion to use John

Browning's autoloader, other than in strictly illegal operations long after protective laws had been passed. However, this piece was much used by outlaw gunners who dealt in waterfowl during the twenties and thirties. It was, and is, a damned heavy hunk of machinery, as are most of today's big-bore choppers—fine for a calculated swing and execution at maximum range, but a handicap in thick brush.

Seventy-odd years of development have produced few radical changes in shotgun conformation. One change is important. The old shooting sticks often featured more drop at heel than is currently popular; straight stocks are now desired, and it is difficult for a shooter weaned on such a model to hit many targets while using the ancient nonpareil. Naturally, one learns to shoot a specific gun, a telling argument against constant replacement. The human being is adaptable.

For sentimental reasons, I award a place in my gun cabinet to a rusty old 16-gauge Eastern Arms single. As a teen-ager, I bought it from Sears for the princely sum of $6.98. Originally, I think, it was graced with a thirty-two-inch full-choked tube, but was soon hacksawed down to twenty-six inches and straight cylinder. The gun remains serviceable, but drop is excessive. I'm sure I couldn't score with it now, but there was a time of glory for that gun.

Back in the twenties, when I was a boy, this mass-produced shotgun collected considerable numbers of ruffed grouse, woodcock, pheasants, ducks, and cottontail rabbits. Each "head of game," because I was then reading *Western Story* magazine and other journals of similar content, is enshrined by a notch on fore end or stock. There are a lot of notches, though I admit to missing more than I hit.

Where fine guns are concerned, straight stocking became popular in the twenties. If you have a vintage piece of great worth dating prior to that time, chances are that drop will be a problem. Actually, this conformation was a phase; there are lots of straight-stocked muzzle-loaders. It would be easy to charge the thing off as a feature of cheap creations, yet the lever-action Winchester '87 was not a cheapie and it certainly qualifies.

In my youth there was a widespread almost paranoid desire for long barrels and full choke. Specialists, among them well-educated market hunters, went to shorter tubes and open boring, but most hunters swore by so-called "goose guns." I had a succession of them, but they kicked the hell out of me, never caused any notable inroads upon the populations of flying game, and were finally traded off or sold. Basically dense, it took me a good many years to learn that woodcock and grouse are close-range targets, best rendered unto possession with a wide-open pipe.

Back in those days, when all the grass was green, I often marveled at old-timers who would say, "Twenty years ago there was a great woodcock cover on Crow Hill, right where all those fine houses are built today!"

Twenty years—to me—was a time span comparable to the age of dinosaurs. It is now worth a rueful chuckle, while I gulp a stirrup cup of Old Fuddlewit, to recall that certain coverts I hunted twenty—and even thirty—years ago have now been converted into suburban developments or industrial complexes. There are factories and private homes and condominiums and blacktop roads dicing a onetime wilderness—and the woodcock are long gone.

In my own town of Shrewsbury, Massachusetts, there is a hillside covered with tidy modern ranch houses—and every owner annually complains about water in the basement. These sterling citizens feel that the town fathers have conspired to inundate them, and a few actually have brought suit to recoup losses.

Nobody will ask me, and I am not about to volunteer information, but that slope was always the wettest place this side of a dismal swamp. It was a magnificent woodcock covert. There were alders and birches, popples, and a few decaying hulks of chestnut trees killed by blight while Wilson was president. There were patches of huckleberries and highbush blueberries and juniper. Ruffed grouse were there, and pheasants sounded off in hazy afternoons. Most important, during the annual trickle-through migration, timberdoodles descended in tawny squadrons. They came because the ground was rich and dank. I have no vendetta against developers, but any destruction of a great shooting ground stirs ancient furies. They killed this covert with housing, and now they cry about a natural phenomenon.

Why, I do not know, but this hillside always was—and is—a gushing fount of clean water. There were always a hundred seeps and springs. Even in a dry October, one slithered through the mud, blessing rubber-bottomed pacs and hoping that a whistledoodle would not flush while one foot was in a bog and the other was sliding off a mossy stone. As far as upland hunters are concerned, this tract is gone, but those of us who once reaped its benefits are maliciously delighted when we hear the sad lamenting of people who built homes in a watercourse and wonder why the government does not legislate against nature.

Today, woodcock hunting is sublime sport, not kill-for-cash. Wisely, federal authorities dictate hunting frameworks, with seasons and bag limits held to a safe minimum. We shoot only in the fall or winter and, where the longbeak is plentiful, we collect a reasonable amount of this renewable resource. There is no unlimited assault on woodcock.

The guns are better. The dogs are better. We have rapid transportation to aid us. Well-educated game biologists are studying woodcock, and their findings will keep us in business. I am an optimist; those of us who love whistledoodle, as well as the bird itself, are in pretty good shape.

# FLIGHTS AND FANCIES    4

*The Mysteries of Migration*

With all our accumulated knowledge, we are still fretfully baffled by the subtle mechanics of migration. Reasons for this annual north–south traffic are obvious enough. Certain birds summer in the cool lands and winter in the semitropics, drawn to climates in which they can best survive, feed, and procreate. One may easily assume that summer residents depart when their chosen food is no longer available and cold weather threatens their very existence. Similarly, rising temperatures in our southland automatically trigger a northward movement to pastures and climates that favor natural reproduction.

These things are basic and universally accepted. How the movement is accomplished, how it is initiated, and how an individual bird navigates with such astonishing accuracy all remain hidden in a fog of conjecture. Even the supposed basics require qualification, because evolution seems to have provided built-in safety valves and a nice margin for error.

Barring unforeseen difficulties, few migratory birds delay a southward migration until food supplies are critically short and cold weather paralyzes the land. Nor, in springtime, do they hesitate to move northward at a predictable time. The biological clock is always ticking away, beautifully attuned, but nature occasionally backlashes and produces abnormal weather conditions; then mankind wonders at a mass exodus or a crippling die-off.

The American woodcock is a true migrant, swarming northward with the vernal equinox and fluttering southward as frost paints northern foliage. A small percentage of these birds defy old custom. Some remain in the Deep South and raise their broods at the edges of Louisiana's piney woods, others proceed up the flyways, peeling off at intervals to become summer residents of various states between the Gulf of Mexico and southern Canada. A vast majority seek the cold lands, touching down in coverts of the central to northeastern United States and in southern Canada.

There is nothing haphazard about this destination. Game biologists, through mist netting, trapping, banding, and release and recovery, have discovered that a majority of woodcock return to the area in which they were hatched. A few mavericks blaze new air trails, but they are exceptions. There is a record of a 'doodle first banded in 1964. It was caught again and released in 1966, and again in 1968—*each time within the confines of the same small northern singing ground.* This longbeak was, at the very least, five years old, since it was mature when first mist netted. There are numerous statistics to prove the existence of three-year-olds, yet—as with so many wild creatures— it is likely that the average 'doodle is pretty lucky to get through a couple of seasons.

Slowly, because the job is time consuming, poorly financed, and often thankless, wildlife management folk are charting arrivals and departures, together with appearances at checkpoints along the way. There are discrepancies, but spring and fall flights generally are punctual. In any given flyway it is quite possible to intercept traffic with surprising accuracy. Unusual weather conditions are the major spoiler, yet nature's goof-offs cause no more than a ripple in the overall ebb and flow.

Biologists may cite the rapidly developing gonads of woodcock in the Deep South, in late winter, plus rising temperatures as triggers of a northward migration. But it is not so easy to detail the restlessness that possesses a northern timberdoodle in late September and early October. Almost certainly the migration is signaled by a slant of sunlight. Nobody knows precisely how such a signal works, but a majority of responsible ornithologists, together with scientists who study pelagic fishes in the sea—now feel that the direction and intensity of sunlight is a prime mover.

Until very recently it was believed that 80 percent of the nation's woodcock population wintered in Louisiana's lush bottomlands. That theory has been challenged by the recognition of at least two major flyways, one east and one west of the Appalachian Mountains. Birds residing east of this barrier winter from the Carolinas southward through Georgia, northwestern Florida, and Alabama or, roughly, in the Southeast.

The second great flyway—possibly most important in point of numbers— funnels woodcock down from Quebec, Manitoba, and the various northern states lying west of the Appalachian chain. There is argument for a third flyway roughly following the Mississippi River. Most of these "western" timberdoodles go into Louisiana and spread out through neighboring Arkansas and eastern Texas.

Banding, and the return of banded birds, indicates some intermingling —but never on a massive scale. Migrating 'doodles are low flyers, unlikely to stray out of paths dictated by terrain features. The longbeak is almost a lighter-than-air flying machine—not a high-performance, high-altitude flyer. He may travel no more than twenty miles a night, or possibly whirl off five times that figure if winds are favorable, the cold is tickling his tailbone, and the biological time clock demands southward movement.

There seems to be no appreciable loss of weight during migration— maybe 10 percent at most—further evidence of a sedate pace with lots of stop-overs to refuel. Aside from the early-fall trickle-through movement, the heaviest flights probably keep birds just ahead of frost and snow advancing southward. No sensible woodcock plans to bend his beak on frozen ground.

Flying speed is a source of endless argument. The fluttering flush of an early-season longbeak can be very slow, but later-flight birds—and even some native birds on second flush—appear to accelerate well beyond the usually accepted 25 mph maximum. I am firmly convinced that many attain speeds of twice the accepted maximum. Bill Pollack agrees. Driving northward in North Carolina one spring morning, he and a companion spotted a timberdoodle flying parallel to the road. For more than a mile, before the highway curved away, that bird matched the car's 55 mph speed. It should be noted that this was a woodcock in transit, not frightened and employing afterburners. They can move.

Since most of our woodcock hunting literature has come out of the Northeast, from Pennsylvania through New England, it is erroneously believed that this is mother-lode country. It is—and it isn't! Michigan's gunners, for example, probably harvest more longbeaks than are taken in any other state. If sportsmen of the Mississippi River delta were as gung ho on whistledoodles as their Yankee cousins, some great bags might be reported. Too often, Southern sportsmen write off the 'doodle as a transient or a second-fiddle day saver.

I have too many amigos in the South to condemn this lack of enthusiasm. Besides, by ignoring woodcock, they ensure more sport for me in a Northern autumn! Quail are magnificent, and I salaam to them, but there is a time of delight with timberdoodles too. The least I can do is report factually, and all facts indicate that more birds stream down the western slopes of the Appalachians than the eastern. There must literally be millions of them.

Because the woodcock flies by night, is secretive and little known to citizens other than ornithologists and upland hunters, arrivals and departures often go unnoticed. Certainly spring migration follows a set pattern, for one can almost state a calendar date upon which they will appear at any point along the flyway.

Tap Tapply suggests an interesting corollary—that woodcock and robins arrive at approximately the same time. It is quite possible that the migrational timetables of the two species coincide. I expect a wave of robins on or about March 12. Woodcock may be in then, but I do not see them because they are cloaked by darkness and hide in thickets during the day.

In 1973, an unusually early spring in Massachusetts, my brother Dick jumped a 'doodle on March 10. That night another friend, Bob Andonian, who spent most of the night rebuilding an airplane in the Bay State's Brookfields, reported much twittering in adjacent apple orchards. These birds soon disappeared, so they were transients flighting northward. At the time, robins were moving through.

Woodcock seem to arrive on schedule year after year, and they proceed to some terminal point that is miraculously imprinted on those strange upside-down brain cells. If a bird was hatched in my back forty, odds are that's the spot he'll call home in a new springtime. If he slit the egg case in eastern Maine, that will be his destination. He will go there and, if a male, will seek an unoccupied singing ground. He, or she, will be accurate in their destination beyond the understanding of man.

Today's great jet transports, their cockpits crammed with intelligent human beings and electronic instruments, follow a beam and a flickering witch's brew of little black boxes to a predetermined point. A woodcock—and every other migrating bird—performs the same miraculous trick, even though the bird relies only on some infinitesimal structure of brain cells, the slant of the sun, and the intermeshing mechanism of something that, for want of a better word, we call instinct. Woodcock are accurate and punctual.

Think about it—and marvel! An atom of flesh, blood, bone, and feathers leaves Georgia or Louisiana in February, heading north. This bird has made one trip southward, having been fledged in the cold northland. Although he or she may be traveling with fellow voyagers, some will descend at intermediate points along the route, and some will flutter much farther into a vast unknown. Yet this sophomore in the game of avian life, having traversed some thousands of miles of hostile, unknown territory, battling gales and frigid weather fronts, will unerringly arrive at a postage-stamp-sized location in a wild hinterland—the place of its origin—and there will establish a summer home.

Following its first encounter at a singing ground and the subsequent production of young in a given area, there may be minor migrations—not nation spanning, but within a region. Since timberdoodles subsist largely on earthworms, any extended drought is certain to cause dispersal of them. This movement may be in any direction until early fall, at which time it will be predominantly southward. Weather conditions are important and may well spur the biological time clock.

Northern hunters are convinced that native birds move first, but this—like the nonsense about large 'doodles being residents, whereas smaller ones are flight—has been proved wrong. Certainly, there is considerable overlap among populations during the fall journey, and sometimes the actual native may delay takeoff until its more northerly cousins have passed through. Always one flushes the laggard, still probing seeps long after the great phalanxes have departed.

I have jumped a woodcock in central Maine during a late-November deer-hunting season when the ground was covered with a foot of tracking snow. The bird may well have been injured during high summer or fall, yet it appeared entirely whole and healthy. Certainly, tarrying much longer in so hostile a climate would prove fatal, and this tardy migrant might already have lost its chance for survival.

There was a belief back in the 1800s that a minority of timberdoodles always wintered over in the North, and that these were the early nesters in springtime. Year-around occupancy at starvation level might be feasible farther south, but it is impossible in Canada, northern New England, or the Upper Peninsula of Michigan. There the entire woodland, its streams, seeps, and potholes, is frozen solid for at least two months, and often for three or four. No whistledoodle could survive.

Normal migration is a trickle-through. Birds begin to move southward as the slanting sun tells them it is time. They are leisurely travelers, perhaps remaining in one location for a week and then working slowly toward the winter's Promised Land of piney woods and bayous. This movement may begin in late September, a parallel to the warbler exodus, but will build to normal peak proportions through October. In central New England, the flight stream is heaviest from early October through the third week of that month, and then tapers off very rapidly.

Generally, birds move through in successive waves but without remarkable concentration. A shooter finds reasonable numbers each day and—occasionally—lucks into that unusual swarm called a flight. This is a phenomenon, far from standard operating procedure, caused by premature snowfall or hard cold.

"Flight" must be defined. Some regard all midseason woodcock as "flight birds," though others reserve the term for a vast number of birds simultaneously dropping into a single covert to provide Olympian sport. The American equivalent of England's "fall of 'cock" happens rarely and is far from usual. Talk to any experienced upland gunner and you will find that he has witnessed few of these mass arrivals. I can recall only one, and it was impressive.

We were in Dover-Foxcroft, Maine, hunting grouse—and there seemed to be no timberdoodles in local coverts during the course of a long day. Trudging back to camp along an old tote road at that witching hour when the tamaracks were etched against a blazing western sky, we ran into a veritable blizzard of woodcock.

There seemed hundreds of them; they fluttered over the alders like a hatch of demented night moths. We enjoyed a pale, early full moon and the light was steadily failing, but we shot until our barrels were hot and collected a fair share of game. Finally, at sunset, it was all over. We decided that the morning would be dedicated to woodcock alone, not grouse.

Unfortunately, the morning proved barren, for the 'doodles were gone. Our alders were liberally undercoated with chalk, yet the legions of sunset had departed before dawn. That was a true flight, undoubtedly pushed southward by some freak of weather or some drastic change in barometric pressure, not by slanting sunrays.

Note that the incoming legions appeared just before sunset. They hadn't been flying during the course of a long day, because this is against woodcock nature. The only logical conclusion is that these birds had been loafing on some brushy plateau in the immediate vicinity and had simply moved out en masse to feed in nearby moist bottomlands just prior to sunset. "Duskers" travel no great distance, though they may well burn up the miles after dark.

Massive flight occurs just often enough to be classic, and it is something to worry about. Panic-induced, it is a phenomenon triggered by some natural catastrophe to the north. Bunched-up, often hurtling southward on gale winds, the travelers are more easily than usual taken by predators, both human and wild. They destroy themselves by colliding with towers, tall buildings, and high-tension lines. They go fast, scared and disoriented. A year of big flights may mean a succeeding season of scarcity.

Ideally, migrations proceed on schedule, with birds whistling southward in well-ordered, well-dispersed numbers. If there is no concentration, a gunner is likely to harbor dark thoughts about scarcity. He needn't worry—with today's international agreements and carefully controlled harvests, woodcock may be the luckiest of all upland flyers. Nobody has offered an adequate estimate of population, but there must be millions upon millions of woodcock. Charley Waterman quips that "compared to the number of other shooters, woodcock hunters are about as plentiful as Rhodes Scholars" —yet these specialists, together with legions of sportsmen who take 'doodles only as targets of opportunity, annually find surprising numbers of longbeaks. If you flush one out of an alder-grown corner, you can be pretty sure that another will be there tomorrow—and maybe a brace on the next visit.

However, Mother Nature often exhibits a sense of humor similar to the Scotsman's idea of a good joke—to half kill a friend. Sometimes the normal trickle-through migration is dislocated by unseasonable weather conditions.

A hard frost or an early blizzard, particularly if that scourge is accompanied by strong winds out of the north or northwest, will send legions of birds fluttering southward. If inclement weather extends over a considerable area, then we get the phenomenon of true flight. In spite of gunner elation, it is bad news.

Limited frosts and snow cover progressing from north to south are different; normal weather conditions push the trickle-through migration, maybe speed it a little, and assure normal gunning. A shooter is wise to study weather patterns to the north of his home grounds. If it's cold up there, and particularly if the wind is strong, gusting out of the north or northwest, he has good reason to believe that his more southerly moist and open ground will be alive with whistledoodles on the morrow. Our longbeak takes a dim view of ice and snow. Still, he is a lightweight in the air, so he likes a tail wind.

The moon phase doesn't matter. I'd like to believe that it does, but unless we can tie it into some corresponding evidence of regional cold and snow, we'd better go with the odds—prosaically accepting the fact that whistledoodles move ahead of arctic blasts and won't waste much time in doing so. Leapfrog jumps are probably short, but birds may well cover seventy-five to more than one hundred miles in a night, especially if borne along by a gusty wind. They are capable of crossing considerable bodies of water. You find them on islands, well off the mainland, perfectly unconcerned and probing for the squirming fodder that will fuel another considerable leg of a long aerial journey.

Many shorebirds are capable of long flights. A 'doodle is all breast, dark and full blooded, a hallmark of the distance flyers: with his abnormally large heart, a whistledoodle has the stamina to go for hours on end. He flies with ease and takes full advantage of favorable winds.

Sportsmen, pseudoscientists who cite no methodical research to support their beliefs, have always looked at the sky and tested the winds and arrived at their own occult conclusions. Rightly or wrongly, gunners of Cape May, New Jersey—a place where woodcock seem to concentrate in great numbers while waiting for favorable winds to help them on a long overwater flight—are convinced that major concentrations will arrive precisely five days after the first hard frost at Albany, New York. Don't ask me why Albany was chosen, but the theory seems to work.

At Cape May the buildup begins in early November and continues through early December. Depending on wind direction and temperature, this influx may continue through much of the twelfth month, and there are reports of birds lingering there after New Year's Day. There are astonishing times when 'doodles are all over the place, landing in supermarket parking lots and resting in the lee of dune grass. Quail dogs go right out of their cotton-picking minds.

Gradually these birds depart, heading south and providing shooting along the way. Vanguards arrive in the Gulf states early in December, and the population then builds steadily to a midmonth peak, which continues through January. Southern shooters take their toll, but it is far less than the attrition in the North in October and November.

Migrating woodcock seem to know precisely where to find forage. How this is so remains a mystery. Granted, abnormal flights may drop in anywhere; they are with us for a few hours, and then—long gone. Trickle-through movement is another thing—then each bird seems automatically to vector into a prime feeding ground.

Count on this: if you have jumped a woodcock out of a certain tangle of grapevines, or under a long-forgotten apple tree, look for another in that spot a day later—or even a year later. They choose areas where forage is plentiful and ignore barren locations. Since many birds-of-the-year cannot have been on this route before, the selection of prime feeding ground is almost miraculous. There are no miracles, so woodcock must have a built-in way of zeroing in.

I have little hot spots that *must* be visited during any upland hunting excursion. Because they have paid off in the past, I know they will prove fruitful in the future. But how does a timberdoodle, fluttering out of New Brunswick in the fall, heading for Georgia or Louisiana, spot tiny pieces of turf along the way and know that each one is good for a banquet of worms?

Perhaps the answer is simple. An airman can tell, by scanning photographs of the ground (and maybe by infrared photography) the precise nature of terrain. Is there any reason why a migrating bird, its luminous eyes reading the landscape, cannot "read" canopy and correctly evaluate coverts where the ground is rich? I think it likely. In any event, migrating timberdoodles make few mistakes.

True flight is another thing. When the big battalions arrive, they may be present for no more than one grand morning and afternoon, after which they will depart. In this case the legions are quite likely to touch down on high ground—the sere and dry uplands where thick birch whips and brambles will slow your swing and where there is no evident food. Flight birds—the true hurry-hurry type—are transients, jittery and prone to run or flush well ahead of a dog. You will find in the bogs their chalk markings, evidently made during the night, but the birds are likely to be far up in dry cover during daylight hours.

During their southward migration, fast-moving birds often pick birch hillsides where they will be sheltered during a rest period. The cover will be thick but will lack appreciable understory. There is no apparent preference for a north or south slope, nor for moist ground in which to probe—although it is worth noting that any north slope should be better, because it is usually wetter than a sun-dried southerly expanse. The only requirement seems to be thick stuff where the ground is reasonably open under a screening canopy.

There is, however, one unusual phenomenon: certain hillsides and plateaus are favored year after year. Although there may be no chalk or other evidence of use, a specific covert may annually play host to the traveling swarms, whereas a very similar piece of nearby real estate may be entirely empty. Is it possible that the flyway is so narrowly defined?

Trickle-through is understandable, and you can pretty safely assume that a small number of birds will be in a good covert at an optimum time—unless somebody has been there before you arrived and pushed them out. The trouble with trickle-through is—just that. Maybe there has been a hiatus in the flow. Occasionally we get into situations that can't be explained, a biological desert at a time when season, temperature, and migrational pattern almost guarantee action.

I defy anyone to choose a single date and declare that woodcock will be plentiful then. Trickle-through or flight, they will be there—or they will not. You can rely on the law of averages and pick the most promising times —which is smart—but you'd better not make know-all pronouncements. The whistledoodle comes and goes when he pleases. Therefore, a man tries to place himself in the flight path to intercept them, but he can't be sure, and he must accept whatever develops. Sometimes that amounts to bitter defeat.

We can be pretty sure that woodcock will be at a certain place at a certain time—provided that the weather obliges. Usually, this means early-season work where the bag will consist of adults and immatures before they have departed for more southerly ranges. During the height of a known migration, we can also expect transients—a hectic ebb and flow, never constant, but sometimes adding up to true flight and a day that will remain in memory forever.

Is it absolutely necessary that we know all of the answers? I like to hunt for treasure. Any sure thing would be boring. It is far better to start each morning with the conviction that *this will be it!*

# WOODCOCK COVER     5

*Timberdoodle's Way-Station*

Everybody says "woodcock in the alders," and that is a belief carefully encouraged by squint-eyed old gunners who know that it contains a measure of truth, plus a lot of nonsense. If they can maneuver the innocents into every muddy, mosquito-ridden thicket in timberdoodle range, then it follows that true disciples will not be bothered while they pursue royal sport elsewhere.

Alder runs are important—in certain places and at specific seasons, such tangles pay big dividends. Nonetheless, they are vastly overrated because the migrating longbeak uses a variety of cover types and often prefers something other than bunched alders.

I know a Cape Cod corner that seldom fails, and it is nothing but jack pine and dry sand bordered by a little stream. The discovery was fortunate; the dog pointed a covey of quail and these little bumblebees fanned out to cross a hardtop road. Holding our fire, we crossed over and searched for singles, only to run into 'doodles galore. Why they were there, only the woodcock know—yet the place is a mother lode and it usually produces in proper season. Jack pine and sand!

Jerry Kissell of Sandwich, Massachusetts, and I used to start every Bay State shooting season in a little suburban covert we called "The Railroad Tracks." It is a small tract of overgrown land bisected by a stream.

There are scattered alders, but more birch and popple, low brush, and an occasional stunted wild apple tree. Towering oaks lift their massive canopy over the thickets, and there are little sidehills choked with highbush blueberry and juniper. The northern perimeter is bounded by a local rail line; hence the name.

Birds usually are there on a Grand Opening, and with the help of a closeworking retriever, Jerry and I often bagged our individual limits within a few hours after sunrise. We've not combined talents in recent years, because Kissell's business took him elsewhere, but this little bonanza still proves worthy when I find it necessary to impress a new companion. Obviously, there is less joy! I have always associated hot corners with specific gunning partners and some of the magic wears off when you go alone, or initiate another sidekick.

Woodcock coverts are personal treasures. Nobody gets to visit my favorites unless he is a very special person, nor do I expect any casual acquaintance to draw maps; such a man would have to be either a dolt or a damned liar. But there is one line of inquiry worth investigating.

Make friends with fanatic brook trout fishermen who are *not* hunters! Wine them, dine them, ply them with exotic feathers to grace their hooks —and then pick their brains! These gentle anglers often run into concentrations of native birds and can tell you precisely where whistledoodles are abundant. Mark it up on a topo map for future reference.

To a hunter, each bonanza is code named, not really as a deception, but according to some romantic sighting, event, or unusual terrain feature. If secrecy is also served, that's a bonus.

Tap Tapply has shown me some heavenly corners in his Winnipesaukee country. I respect his confidence and have never brought newcomers into these beautiful coverts, nor will I do so while Tap and I shoot together. They're his, and I would sooner try to steal his wife—who is worth stealing, by the way—than to run off at the mouth in a company of gunners.

We all name great coverts in an American Indian way, by associating them with something quite natural. You'll cruise the boondocks for a lot of years before locating "The Owl Cover." Tap and his son once flushed a huge owl there. It won't be easy to find "The A-Frame," because it's simply in the general vicinity of such a construction. "The Chicken Coop" is fine too, but there isn't any chicken house; it was there a good many years ago.

Locally, I have "The Sandlot," aforementioned; "The Junkyard," because some forgotten farmer once used part of the area as a dump; "The Cemetery," only since, standing away up on the heights you can see a marble orchard in the distance; and "King's Road," named because a pre-Revolutionary trail, now no more than the suggestion of a trail in a jungle of birch and popple, once snaked over a ridge from central Massachusetts toward Boston.

If there is any point to this nattering, it is that no one of these memory-laden delights is an alder run. One has alders intermixed with birch and poplar; one is scrub pine with a border of oak and wild grapevines; a third is almost all popple, although there are ancient, sucker-grown apple trees haphazardly scattered. We hunt one delicious hillside that is all birch whips, with some of the swaying white beauties grown to maturity. That one has a lot of nasty briar and juniper, too—but whistledoodle is likely to be resident.

Granted, in central Massachusetts we have a few alders that produce woodcock. Mostly, though, great days materialize on high ground where the turf is really too dry, where popples and white birches bar easy progress, and where briars bloody our wrists on every trip. There are scrubby conifers and even scrubbier white oak, a lot of boulders to negotiate and, when the time is right, woodcock en masse.

All right, alders. They are best in the north country, in Canada's Maritime Provinces—in New England, and in Michigan during the first hectic flushes of an early fall season. Whistledoodles reside in this green hell because it offers shade and the ground is well stocked with earthworms. Even then, such a run may be utilized only during the night hours, after which long-beaks will move to higher elevations to loaf from sunrise to sunset.

In extremely hot weather, a condition that often obtains on Opening Day, alders are important because they often edge streams or swampy ground. There are years when timberdoodles must search out the sinks or move elsewhere to ground that is moist and receptive to a beak probing for earthworms. In wet woodlands no such specialization is necessary, so dispersal is correspondingly wide. There is a rather spectacular difference between native woodcock coverts and those chosen by flight birds either trickling through or arriving in a flight.

Any true alder run is at its best when foliage is still terribly thick and the migration has not really begun or is just beginning. At that time, flankers often bag a majority of birds, whereas those hot, mosquito-bitten enthusiasts probing the jungle behind a fine pointing dog or flushing breed get nothing but profanity-inducing snap shots.

In northern coverts, where woodcock shooting has become almost a way of life for upland gunners each October and early November, a mixture of low brush and medium canopy is far more productive than a thicket of alders alone. There are extenuating circumstances, yet a fringe of alders is always better than a great tract of them. Best of all, seek out a nice medley of alder, birch, and popple, with occasional conifers and perhaps a few junipers and clumps of blueberry. If there are some pesky briars, all the better. The ground must be soft unless flight birds are merely resting.

There is another thing to consider: a woodcock likes comfort. He is perfectly willing to parachute into a tremendous tangle of low brush and somewhat higher canopy, but he wants elbow room on the ground. There-

Forgotten apple trees often shelter 'doodles, so they're worth attention.

fore, you are unlikely to be successful in thick grass or other heavy ground cover. Our little whistledoodle wants to patter along *under* the screen, probing soft spots. He likes broad avenues under the world's most exasperating overhead brush. He'll run into a thicket so dense as to defy description, but that's an escape tactic.

Note also that the cover changes with the advancing season. Early in a given shooting period, great locations will be shaded by low canopy. As leaves fall, this heaven-sent sanctuary will be less entrancing and will finally be deserted. Similarly, there are hot corners that simply grow out of productivity. The brush gets too high and pole timber takes the place of low canopy. That's why treasure troves of twenty years ago can become biological deserts today.

Many of us prefer to hunt without gloves, and "chargers" suffer the consequences. A man who goes in like a berserk water buffalo will find his hands and wrists raw and bleeding after a day in the uplands, in spite of the fact that prime locations are reasonably bare under the clutching alders. A snake or a timberdoodle finds no obstacles; man and dog are hampered. Dogs invariably wind up with scratched noses and tailbones. It's rough work for everybody.

Alder edges, particularly where they are thin and there is a mixture of other growth, are worth working. Forgotten apple trees should always be investigated. Popple is promising, and on sidehills where the birch whips are murderous, 'doodles still take up residence. Throughout woodcock range, from north to south, scrub pine intermixed with birch, juniper, and tangled wild grape seems entrancing.

Payoff coverts are not always easily recognized. Soft ground, well populated with earthworms, and with sufficiently screening brush, is obvious. Sometimes you find the telltale chalk and borings but no birds This means they've been there but have moved on. Occasionally, a trickle-through or a real flight will begin at dusk and the legions will depart before sunrise. For some inexplicable reason they may also remain, so chalk is worth investigating. Of course, it is worth noting that other birds leave chalklike droppings.

In migration time, each day is a new adventure; today's bonanza may be tomorrow's bad news. Often a tremendous flight at dusk means a complete absence of birds the following morning. When sunset flights move from local staging areas to feeding grounds, they are likely to fuel up and go streaming southward under cover of darkness—particularly when winds are favorable.

One *hunts* whistledoodles! If the obvious and time-honored locations fail, it is wise to prospect alternative sites. Often, in trickle-through or full-blooded migration—and it doesn't matter whether the woodlands are wet or dry—you'll find daylight concentrations on high ground. If there is no

Heavy foliage and thick growth make early fall shooting difficult.
Paul Kukonen ponders a way through this jungle.

Woodcock often prefer thickets of low stuff, and a gunner is handicapped. Frank Woolner, gun at ready, moves in.

obvious food, the birds must be resting, perhaps soaking up sunshine. They can be in rugged country, as thick as the alders of late September and early October, with lots of birch whips and brambles.

One thing is pretty constant. Longbeaks invariably visit the same locations until such time as that hot corner grows out of adequacy, or hungry developers arrive. That's why woodcock fanciers treasure great coverts; they know the birds will return year after year. Logically, a north slope should be best because it retains more moisture. On the other hand, a southerly expanse will be warmer.

How a whistledoodle recalls well-remembered hot spots remains a mystery; that they do is never contested. There are multitudes of little corners that host no more than one, two, or three at a time—yet they'll always be there during a trickle-through. You take one today and another will be there tomorrow—and still another the day after tomorrow.

This jewel may be nothing more than a stunted wild apple tree at the edge of a birch hillside, a tiny swirl of grapevines at the edge of a swamp, a few popples on a knoll, or an edge where the highbush blueberries fight juniper for living space. If a bird has been there, rest assured that another will arrive. Invariably, such spots are moist and graced by a minimum of

High alders, always good for early-season birds, but far from the best of woodcock cover in peak periods.

Hot corners often include clutching briars that are hat grabbers. Jerry Fiorelli retrieves his fluorescent cap.

low ground cover. Somehow, a migrating 'doodle knows that this is a feeding ground, and flutters in. Find a little hot corner and visit it regularly; you won't be disappointed.

When I was a country boy, and that's a long cast back, cows were fairly plentiful, and a lot of them became half wild during a long and beneficent summertime. Kids went barefoot in that time, and it was not unusual to step in a wet, soft deposit called a cow-flop. For some reason, perhaps reverse psychology, all hinterlands youngsters of my time and place swore that it was particularly good luck to tread on the moist droppings.

Woodcock hunters, if they're wise, may profitably adopt the same superstition. Where cattle have browsed a thickly grown back pasture, there'll be well-trodden paths through alder and birch and highbush blueberries. Indiscriminate manuring probably encourages the propagation of worms, and partial browsing creates little openings that are magnets to traveling 'doodles. If it's just a little muddy, with sprigs of green grass still challenging autumn's frosts, with the crimson berries of black alder and the yellow curlicues of witch hazel readily apparent, then one can expect superb sport.

Thick birch growth may host the fluttering legions.

Be careful, though. Hunting such a spot with Paul Belton, a local friend, I saw a woodcock flush practically under his shoe pacs and hurry away at low level over the stricken blueberry bushes. Just in time, I yelled, "Don't shoot!"

Paul wisely lowered his piece, but he questioned me until I showed him a cow standing right in the line of fire, less than twenty yards away. The critter was shielded from him by a thicket. It turned out that she had just dropped a calf and, hearkening back to some ancient instinct, had chosen to go far into the puckerbrush to do so. We delayed our hunting to alert the husbandman, and so helped to cement an important bond between shooters and landowners.

A wet season can be a good season. Woodcock don't seem to mind rainfall, and you may even find more of them when coverts are dripping. It's tough hunting, yet there'll be a wider dispersal of the quarry. Longbeaks are likely to go twittering out of everything from scrub oak to dwarf pines and suburban apple orchards. In the rain you're more likely to find them right out in the open, on the edges of clearings or in tote roads and grassy trails. They'll be in the sidehill birches, on the high ground—and not as often in the aforementioned alders. If it's wet, then grouse hunters will take more 'doodles as targets of opportunity, and pheasant shooters will find them humping out of reasonably dry swales where patches of low canopy offer little islands of soft ground. The drier the season, the thicker the cover. This seems to be contradictory, but it works with migrating birds.

In the old accounts there is always reference to the shooting of woodcock in cornfields. I think this dates back to July gunning, and is not very important now that we have given the game a summer respite. Cornfields are pretty dry by early fall, so they play host to more ring-necked pheasants and gray squirrels than timberdoodles. Pheasants and squirrels adore corn, but woodcock must find earthworms. A cornfield is not a very good place to seek longbeaks in the fall.

Prime cover naturally varies with the location and season. In the north we think about a mixture of alders, birch, poplar, and a whole host of low brush that shields rich, moist ground. Yet, when the flights sweep down, touching a number of states from our friendly Canadian border to the warm bottomlands of wintertime Georgia and Louisiana, cover changes. There are occasions when the bird is so harried and uncertain that no rule seems to apply.

In 1972 even Cape May shooting was mediocre. Dick Wood, an upland hunter and an old fishing friend of mine, called on three separate occasions to declare that they *hadn't* arrived. I was ready to board an airplane on signal, but that signal never arrived. Evidently 1972's migration was a general trickle-through—the winds were always favorable and woodcock flights never built up.

Such jump-off spots often find birds in covers where earthworms are unlikely, so the best explanation for their presence is a simple stopover to rest. Edward "Spider" Andresen, one of my colleagues at *Salt Water Sportsman*, ran into a considerable number of 'doodles on Martha's Vineyard during the fall of 1973. These had dropped into a brackish, sandy edge near Menemsha Inlet. They'd obviously flown in from the mainland and would shortly set course for Long Island, far across a turbulent stretch of sea.

Dr. Leslie Glasgow feels that 80 percent of the continent's longbeaks winter in Cajun country. Until recently, gunning pressure was light, to the point of nonexistence, and interest still lags. Louisiana's wintertime 'doodle still prefers pretty thick cover, but there are subtle changes dictated by terrain and cover type. During the first hours of darkness, and again just before dawn, Louisiana birds fly to relatively open or cultivated ground where they feast on earthworms. Since there is no more firelighting, and little dusking, hunters go afield in full daylight. Peak season occurs from mid-December through much of January, although a warm winter may see some exodus after the fifteenth of January. A majority of migrants are on their way northward by early February.

Again, as elsewhere in woodcock range, hot corners are those in which the ground is both moist and low-canopied by a mixture of stunted hardwoods, pine, and thorny growth. Runs edged by winter-burned hardwoods adjacent to streams are excellent: look for longbeaks at that point where piney woods march down to bottomlands and surrender to low-lying borders. Characteristically, birds dislike heavy, long grass, but revel in the shade of dwarf holly or other evergreens.

Charles F. Waterman, one of the nation's finest and most widely traveled outdoor writers, tells me that wintering birds in Louisiana seem "to go back and forth to the north a great deal." When there is chilly weather, the locals explain a scarcity by saying that "they've gone up into Arkansas." Charley found good hunting in scrubby evergreen country, and declares that the 'doodles "made some big scratch-ups where they dug around in the needles and the fallen leaves. I went hunting with Grits Gresham near Natchitoches and there were plenty of them there. It was the same spot where Grits made an 'American Sportsman' telecast with Andy Devine. Now it was rainy weather and I assume the worms were easier than usual. Anyhow, we found some birds on open hillsides where a woodcock is a fairly easy proposition. There was always a tree of some sort nearby, but not always enough cover to make shooting difficult. I am guessing that, in dry weather, they would have been nearer the little creeks or 'branches' where the ground would be damp. At both spots I hunted on this trip, bobwhite quail were right with the woodcock."

Northerners very seldom find woodcock on open hillsides, although this does happen in extremely wet weather. Like a striped bass that comes clear of the surface after the manner of an Atlantic salmon, you see maybe one out of a hundred woodcock flush in an open field. Charley mentions "a tree of some sort nearby," so maybe the cover was not as open as his account indicates.

"In much of that country," he continues, "there are patches of thick brush, often thickets fifty or sixty feet across, and the woodcock are often found in them. They will move around considerably over a small area when worked with dogs." In his excellent book, *Hunting Upland Birds*, Charley declares, "A woodcock isn't going to take out and leg it a mile or so across hill and dale, but it will go trundling around a thicket like a toy bird with its spring winding down."

That's a nice appreciation, and I wish I'd thought of it first!

There are few dedicated woodcock hunters in the South. There, the bobwhite quail is supreme and some gunners actually get caustic when their dogs point a 'doodle. Many, in fact, do not even recognize the species as a game bird. In Florida, some longbeaks are found in the northern coverts around Tallahassee and in the Panhandle. There are lots of wintering birds in Georgia and Alabama, in Mississippi, in Arkansas, and eastern Texas, but only a few enthusiasts seek them. Even in Louisiana, shooting pressure is

Charles F. Waterman, with a well-soaked Brit, admires a northern Louisiana bird. *Photo by Charles F. Waterman*

light. This bird ranges across half a continent from north to south, yet enjoys wild adulation only north of the Mason-Dixon line, or a short jog southward. Virginians seek timberdoodles as ardently as do the gunners of my cold land.

Claude Rogers, of Virginia Beach, Virginia—a surf-casting authority, a woodcock hunter, and a Southerner I admire because he tempers a tendency to be highly opinionated with a wry sense of humor—finds lots of birds each fall. Claude says that I talk funny, and I maintain that his drawl is exaggerated Jeb Stuart. We're both right.

Rogers is pretty cynical about the accuracy of outdoor writers, but doesn't alibi his own expertise under duress. He declares, "Infallibility rises in direct proportion to the amount of alcohol consumed. I get more and more infallible as a night wears on and the bourbon disappears!" Can anyone say nay?

George Bird Evans, a respected outdoor-writing colleague who lives in Bruceton Mills, West Virginia, annually harvests 'doodles over his classic Old Hemlock setters, and George has written some very stirring prose about woodcock and grouse. He often hunts in the Canaan Valley area, which is reputed to be absolutely tops in West Virginia, but he has sampled a wide range of coverts.

C. P. Wood of Falling Waters, West Virginia, is another enthusiastic 'doodler and outdoor writer. Woody tells me that his eastern panhandle

Woodcock may be in relatively open country when it's wet in
Louisiana. Charles F. Waterman approaches a Brit on point.
*Photo by Charles F. Waterman*

Thickets forever plague woodcock hunters. Bob Anderson moves in to flush an anchored whistledoodle in Louisiana. *Photo by Charles F. Waterman*

section is not supposed to be the best woodcock cover in the state, "but I never have reason to complain.

"During fall seasons such as the past two, we have had excellent shooting. Greatest concentrations are ensured by a sudden, hard freeze to the north of us. This will put birds into almost every suitable covert by the hundreds, and they will hang around until a local freeze hardens the ground —and then you can't buy one.

"Best shooting usually occurs between November first and December first. That's a rough estimate, because weather conditions dictate. In 1973 we didn't get many birds until mid-November, and a grand flight poured into our coverts during the first week of December. That's admittedly unusual.

"Here, in the eastern edge of West Virginia, we are not supposed to be on the main route of 'doodle migrations, and state game people will tell you that a majority of birds go down the groove in the Appalachians. However, I think there is also a sizable percentage of woodcock that come down the eastern side of the mountains. I also suspect that these birds run later than those in the major flyway.

"During the first week of December 1973, I found wonderful concentrations. My Llewellin setter, Kate, would point a 'doodle and we would drop it. Sometimes two or three more would get up at the shot, and I made several doubles if you want to call such a staggered rise a double. Many of these birds were in relatively open fields and I found myself wishing for an autoloader as there were times when I might have dropped four within a couple of seconds—if I could hit them. It reminded me of snipe shooting back in the days when we really had snipe."

On northern breeding grounds, sportsmen often spend the spring season hunting—not to kill, but to admire. It starts on cold singing grounds, then on stream banks. Since an upland hunter usually is a man of all seasons, a trout-fishing expedition may be interrupted to investigate singing or nesting longbeaks. Rising squaretails are momentarily forgotten when a woodcock flutters skyward or a hen is seen marshaling her brood of four tiny gnomes.

Fishermen may be excused for daydreaming about slopes where alders are sparsely evident among white birches and aspiring poplar. For a few minutes, in June warmth, one declares a secret moratorium to fix the spot in mind and to promise a return when red maples are flaming. In our north country, trout, grouse, woodcock, and white-tailed deer comprise a holy quartet, and no one of them is more important than the other except as a season dictates.

Film star Andy Devine hunts Louisiana woodcock during an ABC-TV "American Sportsman" production. *Photo by Grits Gresham*

George Bird Evans, plus Old Hemlock Dixie and Briar, emerge
from a choice Canaan Valley, West Virginia, covert. *Photo by
Kay Evans*

Often, early prospecting is worthless, its joy lying only in anticipation.
Slopes that appear to be sure things in springtime (and may look quite as
good in October) may draw no migrants. The trickle-through follows old
and established routes; hence a gunner is reluctant to disclose way-stops he's
discovered. Evidently, aside from harried and wind-blown formations dropping in to "any port in a storm," navigation is precise.

Nonetheless, it is a signal triumph to discover a new bonanza by reading
sign. If one returns to that promising location in the fall and finds it well
stocked with tawny flyers, delight is almost impossible to conceal. Meet
another upland shooter in such a paradise, and he'll be cordial—yet a hearty
greeting and exchange of information never conceals a glint of outrage. You
sense this fellow thinking *How the hell did you blunder into MY covert!*

There is a good deal of deception and gentle espionage involved where
local sharks conspire to retain secrets and where casual acquaintances search
for clues. Parking one's car on the shoulder of a state road that happens to
border a fine slope is tactically unsound—the automobile will be recognized
and conclusions will be drawn. Strategy dictates motoring into a hidey-hole
well screened by foliage and terrain. In extreme cases it is better to trudge
a country mile over a ridge from a parking site than to disclose a hot corner.

C. P. Wood, of Falling Waters, West Virginia, with Llewellin setter and woodcock. The over-under is a customized Franchi with 22-inch open-bored barrels. *Photo by C. P. Wood*

One chooses one's companions with care and maintains a discreet silence outside the magic circle. But all of us find it pleasant to initiate a new friend, and there is standard operating procedure for this.

A prospective gold mine may lie one mile from the point of departure, but it would be naive to go directly there via known road nets. The great trick is to circle, to consume considerable time in backtracking, bumping over secondary roads and farm tracks. It may be essential to show a friend grand shooting, but when he describes this veritable jewel of cover to another party over evening cocktails, it will be soul satisfying to hear him mutter, "I still don't know where the hell we were!"

Naturally, this doesn't apply to old cronies in the uplands. Usually, woodcock addicts hunt two by two, and they are as close-mouthed as a revolutionary cell plotting to overthrow a government. Each smidgeon of information is carefully digested and fed into mental computers.

"Harry Wright's station wagon was parked back of Howland's orchard on Thursday. You suppose he found birds on that popple slope?"

"Can't shoot 'The Crossbow' on Saturday. Too many damned pheasant hunters around, and somebody would spot the car."

"Ludlow told me he jumped a bunch of 'doodles yesterday when he went to fetch a calvin' cow out of the back forty. I asked him to keep his mouth shut about it."

Cover can be the world's best—and still fail. During a fall migration, woodcock are mercurial—here now, and suddenly gone. This can happen in prime time, as I discovered to my discomfiture one day while trying to guide Johnny Marsman to success in four of the finest of whistledoodle bonanzas. Johnny was then marketing and advertising manager for Savage Arms Company, and I was doing some free-lance work for him. Naturally, I was eager to show off and find the boss more woodcock than he'd ever seen.

Paul Kukonen and I set it up. We picked a date "guaranteed" to be ideal. We had Paul's setter bitch, Lizzie, and there are few better performers on 'doodles. We repaired to a central Massachusetts covert where success had never been measured in anything other than limits and numbers of birds flushed.

It was just about the worst fiasco I have ever experienced!

Although it was late October, temperatures climbed to July levels. That shouldn't have hurt, because some of the finest timberdoodle shooting in this world occurs under conditions reminiscent of a sauna bath.

Tom Gresham of Natchitoches, Louisiana, cautiously moves into position as his pointer locates a 'doodle in thin piney woods. *Photo by Grits Gresham*

Paul Kukonen moves ahead of his setter, Lizzie, on point in a
Massachusetts covert.

But there just weren't any birds! Sweating through four grand coverts during the course of an entire day, bonanzas that—twenty-four hours before —had been loaded with longbeaks, one lonely flush was the sum total. Kukonen harvested that longbeak with an impossibly long shot, but Johnny and I never pressed a trigger.

Hot, exhausted, and humiliated, we left Marsman in the humid sunset and headed home. Zipping down a blacktop at some sixty mph, a rejuvenated hornet flew right into my left ear and I came within inches of wrecking the carryall.

When he'd quit shouting and we'd leveled off, Kukonen growled, "After *this* trip, anything we do will be a comeback!"

In retrospect, we were lucky. The way things trended that day, it's a wonder I didn't shoot Marsman, break a leg—and then kill all hands in a hornet-induced automobile accident.

It would have been a tragedy to lose Lizzie that way.

# THE EASY MARK     6

*Gunner Strategy Afield*

Any halfway decent upland marksman ought to tumble three out of five woodcock flushed over a solid point. Maybe more—because what's so difficult about a close-range target that flutters toward the alder tops, hesitates for a moment, and then jogs off like an absentminded butterfly? Nothing at all, yet those of us who are addicted to whistledoodles recall too many occasions in which the stereotype flush has been replaced by something right out of a witch's cauldron. The little guy can be easy—and he can be very tough. There are complications.

The easy mark charge is leveled by gunners who specialize in other, faster flying game—and who still shake their heads when a supposedly simple 'doodle goes weaving over the canopy after a few loads of bird shot have disturbed nothing but birch twigs and space.

It is also said, with a slight measure of justification, that northern grouse hunters are nothing but woodcock hunters in disguise. The longbeak, according to this train of thought, is relatively plentiful, lies well to a mediocre dog, and is easy to harvest. Therefore, the classic upland gunner wears a grouse feather in his cap, but actually seeks timberdoodles.

I will argue neither point, since both are valid, but I suggest that generalities are dangerous. A woodcock *is* an easier target than a grouse—usually! Some professed grouse hunters quit the field after timberdoodle flights have passed through, but more seek *both* as targets of opportunity. It would be idiotic to ignore seasonal abundance.

And then, of course, there are folk who count the woodcock the finest game bird in this world. They follow the flights from frosty Canadian provinces down to the piney woods of our Gulf Coast; they breed grand pointing dogs, and they select firearms that are joys to behold, delights to handle, and deadly in execution. Such men—and women—become slightly apoplectic when a know-all type declares that the longbeak is easy to bag.

If the detractor adds that woodcock are inedible, then your true aficionado assumes a livid complexion—and fisticuffs are possible even in polite society. On this point I am adamant: there is nothing more delectable than tender, well-prepared timberdoodle on toast, baked, broiled, or fried. Still, I know that human beings are sharply divided on this issue. You either hate woodcock as food, or extol them as a gourmet's pièce de résistance. There is no middle ground.

This, by the way, is no Johnny-come-lately opinion. Captain Bogardus wrote, "It is still a pretty hard bird to shoot, for now it flies like a bullet, and zigzags and twists about among the close-standing stems, going for an opening through which to make a straight flight. The woodcock flushed in cover always goes for an opening; the ruffed grouse never does, but sets sail for the closest and densest part. Now, when the woodcock is going swift and twisting among the stems of the saplings, he is very easy *to miss*. It is," he added, "one of the richest morsels on the table that the woods and fields supply." Amen.

Hunting whistledoodles without a dog is a journey into frustration—you can do it, but you won't be very successful. Annually, grouse, quail, and pheasant shooters take a few that are practically stepped upon before their hectic flushes. Even where a discerning sportsman notes chalk and fresh probing, it takes much beating of the bushes to jump a 'cock. This little gnome lies close, and you almost have to kick him out of cover. The jump shooter probably walks by ten birds for every one that a good dog would locate.

Ideally, you have a pointing dog or a close-working flusher-retriever that will operate within optimum range. Lacking a canine companion, you simply visit little hot corners that have always hosted 'doodles, and you tramp around and hope for action. At flush you'll always be off balance, the sun will be in your eyes, and there'll probably be too much foliage for comfort. Did somebody say they were easy?

With or without a dog, woodcock hunting is early-season sport. There will be steaming heat and a screen of leaves that have resisted the first killing frosts. A bird may well get up at your boot tips, and those early ones often twitter away like ailing helicopters. They flutter valiantly, heading for the light at the top of the canopy, and then zigzag off in various directions.

Hot, early-season shooting is hard on dogs, so they delight in cool-off streams or water holes.

The trouble is—*time!* You can get on at ten feet, or even twenty. At that range a charge of fine bird shot would mangle the target. Tracking, perhaps muttering words that would be censored in anything other than today's underground press, you wait for the clean shot at perhaps twenty yards.

In early-fall woodlands a timberdoodle can disappear, swallowed up by screening foliage, in split seconds. The few that tower into a hostile sky are well remembered—because they are so few. At this time of year a hunter's success ratio nose-dives because he just can't get on the target before the bird has evaporated. Desperation shots at the line of flight sometimes succeed; more often they are futile.

Even if the cover is relatively open, a zigzagging woodcock is a pretty deceptive mark. He looks so easy that there is a tendency to get overconfident, to hold right on and belt a slow pigeon. In the first place, that vertical flush introduces problems: the average gunner finds it natural to swing horizontally in leading, but it goes against the grain to sweep a piece up (or down). In any form of wing shooting, the toughest pokes are those at a target towering rapidly or diving earthward.

Traditionally—and don't be too eager to accept tradition as infallible—

A great excuse for missing—a sapling caught by the full charge of small shot. Tracking a bird, one never sees roadblocks.

a woodcock flushes at close range, towers slowly (if erratically), and levels off at the tops of birches or alders. You take him at the peak of that ascent, and it works—but not always. Unaccountably, just as a trigger finger looses the charge, that amazing little rascal side-slips or changes direction. A timberdoodle always zigs when he is supposed to zag. Some seem to hang in the air like bewildered helicopters; a few always go off like unguided missiles, twisting through the brush. And there will be curious characters that practically knock your hat off, and then land twenty feet away.

Short-flight birds are confusing. They often plummet immediately after a shot has been fired, and the gunner has every reason to believe that he has scored. Actually, as is shortly made apparent by a second flush, the 'doodle has simply decided to parachute into cover. Some will lie so close that you won't believe it. I will never quit shaking my head over an object lesson I had on this.

Hunting without a dog, and therefore not really seeking woodcock, I had approached a little tangle of woodland grapevines that annually host 'doodles. Gun up at port arms, I prospected this treasure chest, tramping back and forth. Nothing happened, so I got careless and lowered the piece.

A woodcock promptly fluttered out of the dry shards beneath my boots, brushing my face in flight. Frantically, I tried to get on—and thought that I might have succeeded just as this plump little target passed through the yellow crown of a stunted beech.

I went down there and searched diligently, but with no success. Stubbornly, feeling that I'd better take another line of sight, I went back to the grapevine and tried to reconstruct the scene. While standing there, completely unprepared, another woodcock launched out of the same tangle and, of course, I missed again—gloriously.

Those were classic sucker shots, yet I blew both because all my controls were crossed, mentally and physically. Few 'doodles move out like a rocketing grouse, but split seconds are important when a clumsy gunner has to rearrange his hands, place an index finger on a safety catch, mount the piece, and snap off a reasonably well-directed shot at a jinking target in the shadow and shine of autumn foliage.

There are lots of good reasons for missing, among them that which I call, for want of any better term, the ego factor. One dotes on impeccable performance in the presence of one's peers. Therefore, if Tap Tapply happens to be standing right behind me when a whistledoodle climbs toward the birch tops, I want to nail that tawny target and make it look easy. So, of course, I get too deliberate, probably overcorrect—and miss like the sorriest of beginners. Tap will be diplomatically silent, but I talk to myself for an hour thereafter.

Post-miss breast beating always amuses Tapply, who maintains that I spend at least a half hour crying over every bird that escapes. Admittedly, there is a stereotyped procedure. Initially, I list all sorts of reasons for missing—caught off balance, target lost in the sun, a thicket that snatched at a swinging gun, poor reloads, or maybe perspiration in my eyes. I am, frankly, furious, and it takes a little while before I stop this nonsense, chuckle, and tacitly admit, "You old rascal, you just missed!"

Don't discount the ego factor; it's hard to beat, because we're all grandstand players in a sense. Simply blot out everything in the red and gold world other than that little zigzagging beauty. Swing the gun smoothly—and take him. I know it's easy to say.

You won't see many tables computing proper lead on flying woodcock, because there is a general misconception about the flight speed of 'doodles. Some dubious authorities declare that 25 mph is top speed, but they cannot have spent many seasons in the birches and alders. Some birds travel much slower, yet the twisters of late October and November fly like hell. Keep in mind Bill Pollack's clocking of a woodcock at 55 mph—and it is well to remember that this 'doodle wasn't startled, he was simply in transit.

As in any wing shooting, a gunner must lead the target, or he'll miss. Since most upland shooters employ the swing-through technique, often called snap shooting, leading has never been emphasized. It is there, and it will be greater or lesser depending upon the speed and the angle of the mark. Most misses are due to stopping the gun and throwing a shot string behind a fleeting bird. It is always better to be ahead than behind, and this isn't rhetoric, because the shot string is a long sausage of pellets. If the leading edge misses, following pellets may well zero in.

I do not know why, but there exists a common misconception that a smoothbore's entire charge arrives simultaneously; it does not. It is a definite string of shot, and nattering away about pattern at a specific range only bolsters the misconception.

The so-called patterning, or circular imprinting of pellets at a given distance, cannot be challenged. Confusion arises because laymen are seldom advised that pellets arrive individually, not en masse. Envision the shot string as just that, say a six-foot sausage of shot, dispersing and occupying more air space as it travels. You catch a fast-flying bird with no more than a small portion of the string. The shot pattern on a stationary target is deceptive, because you'll not be shooting at sitting ducks in the boondocks.

This, of course, is one major reason why big-bore shotguns are more efficient than small-bores—they throw more pellets, and so the string is longer, wider, and denser. A question arises: how much is enough? Certainly 1⅛ ounces of shot thrown by a low-based 12-gauge shell is sufficient on woodcock. I happen to think that ⅞ of an ounce propelled by a low-based 20-gauge tube is excellent; below this we will wrangle.

Gunning tactics change with the season and, in the North, there is rapid change during October. With few exceptions, the early poke will be at a close-range mark, swiftly disappearing in a sea of foliage. There will be handicaps not usually associated with upland shooting, such as unbearably hot weather. One's backyard tomato garden may be withered by frost, but summer fights a valiant delaying action on sunny mornings and afternoons. A man sweats for every bird he pockets, and must therefore dress accordingly.

Early 'doodles usually lie tighter than those of midseason and seem to be slower in flushing. You don't find as many fidgety little cusses who run ahead of a dog and jump wild. They don't have to, because the screening brush is a major ally. Shots will be taken at fifteen to twenty yards, or they won't be taken at all. Indeed, there is a temptation to blast away at twenty feet—a sorrowful mistake.

The early whistledoodle is almost always met in a brushy jungle where mosquitoes still hum and spider webs tickle. The birch aphids will plague you and the ground will be soft, perhaps splotched with chalk and the unmistakable evidence of boring. A good covert will be thick, but there'll be no carpet of growth on the earth itself. A man must push through an assortment of thorny, cast-iron brush that will constantly impede his way, snatch off his hat, and prevent the rapid swinging of an open-bored shotgun.

Presently a dog makes game and quickly locks up—solid. You know that a woodcock is pressed against the earth just ahead of those bulging eyes and quivering nostrils, maybe hidden under a yellow bower of dying fern, or perhaps all but invisible against a latticework of fallen leaves and sparse grasses. Often a canny dog will close to within scant feet of the hidden quarry and, occasionally, if you're sharply observant, it is possible to locate the squatting game—first by the glitter of its eyes.

Now there is a matter of strategy. Tradition holds that a 'doodle, half blind in bright sunlight, will head for an opening, seeking light. Certainly they gravitate toward openings, yet I think this has little to do with vision deficiency. It is wise to gauge all escape routes while moving in with gun at port arms. There won't be much time to act. Two men can cover the exits better than one, but three begin to approximate a crowd—unless the third man acts as a flanker.

Where two or more men hunt together, simultaneous shots at wildly flying birds are inevitable. Often both place pattern on target, yet neither is aware that the other has fired. No problem, where gunners are close friends and reasonably forgiving. Conflict arises when a gung-ho type always asserts that the mark he shot at is his, because it dropped at the bark of his gun. A companion may have touched off at the same instant, the reports blending into one. How often have we all tumbled a bird, enjoyed a flush of pride, and then registered astonishment as a companion also pulled a smoking spent shell out of his piece?

Very possibly I once robbed Kukonen of a nice and difficult double. Although I'm sure he made both shells count, I'm equally sure that I hit the second bird at the precise instant he did. It was a curious situation.

We were working a heavily brushed slope and Lizzie happened to lock up in a solid point while he and I were on opposite sides of her position. Following the bell (really the sudden silence), we both converged on that point. I caught a fragmentary glimpse of Kukonen approaching my right front, another flash of Lizzie pointing between us—and then a 'doodle went spiraling skyward!

Paul was just a blur in the brush, and I suddenly wondered if he knew I was right in his line of fire. We both wore fluorescent blaze orange caps, but that was a real jungle. I dropped to one knee and heard him punch out a single shot. Split seconds later I saw a woodcock weaving back over the birches, well up and clear. Thinking that my amigo had missed, I swung quickly, fired, and the 'doodle collapsed. Somehow you always know when you are on. I hit that bird.

Kukonen hit it too, but I never heard him shoot because the two reports were simultaneous. It transpired that there was a brace (I only saw one), and Paul's first shot string had tumbled a bird flying in the opposite direction. He then turned and, together, we blasted the second. Too bad I had to muscle into the act, but there was no way to know. Fortunately, neither of us was seeking medals for valor, and Lizzie cared not at all. She simply flash pointed each dead bird and then ignored them as unworthy of further attention.

As a sidebar, here, I will tell you how to make a grown man cry—and it is a delicious bit of business, especially if the victim is a good friend, very capable and proud of his skills with a shotgun. Picture this:

Two men are moving in on a solid point. At flush, your gun is absolutely tangled in clutching alders or birch whips, so there is no chance of getting off a shot. Meanwhile, the bosom buddy consummates one of those dream pokes, a clean kill at forty yards, curving—one of the finest shots this world has ever witnessed!

Break your gun. Walk out nonchalantly, blowing nonexistent smoke through the barrels, and inquire, "Did you shoot, too?"

On point, where there are no obvious difficulties, one gunner usually is given preference. It is his chicken, until such time as he misses. Where shooters of equal skill work together, it is customary for the dog's owner to take that first bird, after which positions will alternate. Often in hard going—which is most of the time in woodcock hunting—nothing can be planned because visibility will give the poke to one or another of the converging shooters.

The flanker strategy is very important when working a border of alders or heavy birch growth. One man follows the dog, if it is a pointing breed, while the other parallels the edge so that he can get a clean shot at any target bursting out of low canopy into a wide-open sky. Where flushing dogs are employed it is feasible—and often profitable—to send the dogs in and remain outside. Granted, some 'doodles will flash away at low altitude in the brush, or go twisting off out of range, but a fair percentage are sure to offer a main chance.

An early-season bird is apt to lie so tight that, literally, you have to nudge him out of hiding. Then he'll flush dramatically, and the soft buffeting of wings will be laced with that wild twittering of air escaping through primaries. He'll be very close—perhaps brushing your face as he spirals toward the top of the canopy. With any kind of luck, this bird will level off, according to tradition, and then set a relatively straight course over the treetops. Hopefully, if early-fall foliage affords an opening, it is possible to wait for that second in which the target attains ideal range and has straightened out. Unhappily, birds do not always fly a traditional pattern.

This crazy character is likely to boil out like a bee-stung bat, describe a tight circle around your head—and land twenty feet away! Others proceed according to plan, but instead of leveling off, as any respectable woodcock should, they take evasive action. A timberdoodle is far from fast, but he's maneuverable. A grouse may be likened to a high-performance fighter plane,

Woodcock flushing at close range, with gunner swinging.

Heavy foliage demands quick shooting—and a measure of luck. Dean Clark moves in as his setter points.

whereas a whistledoodle is a lightweight stunt job. He can move, when that's necessary, but sudden wing-over turns, abrupt changes of speed, and the old falling leaf caper regularly confound gunners.

Nobody is more pathetic than a deadly wing shot who suddenly switches from fast-flying grouse to 'doodles. All of his instincts scream for the fast overtaking swing, and he places charge after charge yards ahead of aerobatic, slow-moving longbeaks. When this man goes back to grouse he'll groan at shot strings far behind their rocketing marks!

Although grouse and woodcock are heavenly twins of the uplands, and are often taken together, there are differences in their prime cover. Much depends on weather and ground conditions, but as a general rule of thumb, hot corners for one bird will not produce the other in comparable numbers. If a man zeroes in on whistledoodles, he'll harvest the stray pat. Similarly, the grouse hunter runs into a scattering of longbeaks. Double-threat shooters take advantage of terrain to collect a mixed bag—and accept the occasional pheasant silly enough to boil out of thick brush.

If there's a trick to early-season shooting, it's concentration. Barring the swinish killer instinct that demands a score even though a whistledoodle is blasted into bloody nothingness at twenty feet, you will lose many that simply disappear in a green sea of alders and birches. Bar-nothing killers are never popular among conscientious shooting men, but the occupational hazards of Opening Day are accepted even by classicists. There are, regardless of season, unexpected happenings.

I hunted with an excellent gentleman who was meeting whistledoodles for the first time. He was eager, and so he shot too fast. Each charge went home, but then he wept about the quick kill that shredded a grand game bird. In short order he became too cautious—and became a complete loser. There is a nice compromise: let them go, unless you can score at practical range, say fifteen yards at a minimum. That's only forty-five feet.

Beginners in the uplands, unfortunately including a few outdoor writers who should know better, stress the need for split-second action on grouse or woodcock. The hurry-hurry approach is a mistake. A killer will move rapidly, but never trust to the luck of an ill-directed shot string. Luck is for the birds—it keeps them very much alive!

Skeet and trap shooting have been touted as training grounds for field shooting, and I agree that they help. Both games acquaint a shooter with his gun and teach him to swing and lead. It does not necessarily follow that a fine skeet or trap shooter will be deadly in the uplands—or that a superb field shot can wipe the eyes of comrades in clay-bird competition. Either can be a duffer in a new arena, because there is a diametrically opposed difference in the disciplines.

The trouble with field shooting, as opposed to white-rock competition, is that nobody yells "pull" in the birch whips—and there is no "grooving" a target. Most important, American skeet and trap shooting fosters a gun-at-shoulder stance while calling for a bird. Nobody does this in the back country, so the practice is artificial. Europeans generally shoot from the international position, with the gun's butt at the athlete's pelvic ridge. This is more honest, if the game is intended to approximate field sport.

I am a skeet shooter, but not a very good one, because I insist on shooting from the international position. That's the way originators of skeet planned it, since they envisioned a game to hone the talents of grouse hunters, not the quail now emblazoned on the skeet symbol. Even if quail had been considered, the gun-at-shoulder stance remains nonsense. We just do not hunt this way.

By all means, embrace skeet as a trainer, but resist the siren song of good scores assured by the gun-at-shoulder stance. Skeet colleagues will beat you, but they won't do better in the field if you have pointed toward the quick swing from port arms. That's the way it is when all the blue chips are down in the whispering wilderness. Nobody calls for a bird, and there is no grooving anticipated flight. You'll either compensate, or you'll go hungry.

In skeet, an experienced gunner finds Station Eight no problem. It requires fast gun handling, but the clay need only be centered. If a smoothbore is swinging properly, no lead is required. In the puckerbrush, woodcock often drive straight overhead to offer the same shot—and I miss a lot of them. Alibis? Well, there's always a lot of screening brush or other handicaps.

Making a motion picture with Kukonen, who was handling the camera, I had a classic Station Eight at a 'doodle in relatively open poplar growth. Paul flushed the bird off to my right, and I turned at his shout to see it boring straight overhead in a clear blue sky. Everything was right, with one minor exception—a poplar I failed to see.

The charge of eights struck it solidly, and the whole crown of that damned tree came down, the butt smacking me solidly in the forehead. For an awful moment I thought the gun had blown up or the woodcock was shooting back!

Paul wasted no sympathy. In fact, he ranted like a fishwife, berating me for missing. Like all motion-picture photographers, he could hear nothing but dollar bills departing as film whirred through a camera adjusted to shoot slow motion. This means sixty-four frames per second, or more, and you can run through a considerable wad of money exposing 16 mm color in a segment that will wind up on the cutting room floor. That's one of the reasons why a fine outdoor motion picture is expensive.

I recall another blown Station Eight. Tap Tapply and I had repaired to a New Hampshire birch slope just after sunup. Tap's Brittany, Bucky, jumped a longbeak that came back right over my head. It should have been the easiest score in the world, but two things happened. First, the 'doodle and a robin seemed to be flying in formation, one behind the other. Second, the sun was in such a position that both birds appeared blood red. I hesitated —just long enough to make no shot at all.

To be reasonably successful in woodcock hunting, one must be well balanced and cat quick in getting on. It is easy to mouth banal platitudes about an easy mark, but just try to score with a lame leg or any other infirmity that retards swift, coordinated action: you'll be flummoxed. I lost most of a good season with a pulled ligament in a right knee—it didn't hurt much, but I couldn't react.

On one trip into the grand coverts around New Hampshire's Lake Winnipesaukee, I quietly watched Tapply miss four birds in succession. They weren't that tough and—though I managed to remain silent while biting the hell out of a good pipestem—the jaunt had somehow turned sour. Although Tap forever disparages his own ability and denies any skill in scattergunning, he is actually an accomplished wing shot, a man I would pit against the best. Later, back in the cushioned comfort of our car, with Bucky hunkered down in the back seat noisily licking his crown jewels, I demanded an explanation. "What happened? You may be a lousy shot, as you claim, but you're not *that* bad!"

He chuckled and ruefully admitted a handicap. "Don't tell Muriel, because I want to get through the season before I see a doctor, but I popped a hernia last week and the thing bothers me. I'm favoring myself and the birds are taking advantage."

Just that. If you have a pulled muscle, a sore foot—anything distracting and painful—then it will be difficult to move swiftly during those fractured seconds when a bird is in the air. The need for sharp reflex action and smoothly coordinated muscles becomes apparent when any little cog in the chain slips.

I didn't tell Muriel. She's a registered nurse, and all nurses are given to undue worrying about people they love. Still, my friend was wrong—he was troubled and couldn't camouflage the fact. When Tapply misses three or four birds in a row, I need no ESP to figure that something has backlashed. Usually he weeps bitter tears about his lack of skill—while he wipes my eyes on tough shots. Tap never berates himself, as I do, after a miss; he seems to regard this as normal and the direct hit an exception. I hold this attitude truly exceptional, for most of us are big in the alibi department.

Ed Pease of Brookfield, Massachusetts, ties all of his excuses into dog work. When he blows a perfectly delightful chance, he forever mutters about handicaps engendered by the "handling" of his fine Brittany. The dog, I think balefully, was on solid point and handling consisted of moving in, kicking the woodcock out of cover, and shooting it down! Unfair, perhaps, because fine sportsmen *are* somewhat distracted by dog work, particularly when they're hosting visiting firemen.

Pease doesn't miss that many, yet I grin secretly as the dog-handling alibi is trotted out. Like all of us, he later admits that he simply threw a shot string ahead or behind, or got one foot stuck in a mudhole. He's accurate, and fine scattergunners are proud of their talents. It hurts to admit the gunner error that lets a bird go weaving over the canopy whole and free. I cry a lot. Someday I'm going to write a book called *1,000 Alibis*. If it's a success I'll recall another thousand for a sequel.

Weariness is a major contributor to failure. If a man is out of shape and tires easily, if his shotgun is too heavy for a long haul, if the weather is unbearably hot—as so often it is during the first weeks of a new season— then fatigue will take its inexorable toll.

The dogs work nobly and point like statues. Timberdoodles depart like bats in hell, zigzagging over the birches. Perspiring copiously, cruelly scratched by briars, tickled by everything from spider webs to aphids, and convinced that clutching brush is fiendishly placed to defeat a shotgun's swing, we find lots of empty air for futile charges of shot. It's easier to miss than to hit.

A typical day is not always that of the tale tellers. In the first place, there is no need to arise at 4:00 A.M., as we do in duck-hunting season. Whistledoodle is a gentleman's bird: he'll be there at 10:00 A.M. and will be obliging right up until sunset. It is quite possible to go in after some measure of wetness has been burned off the underbrush, to hunt comfortably and well until noon—and then to take a short siesta for lunch. Midafternoon hours are productive, but who needs to scour the brush until moonrise? If birds are there, full daylight is an adequate time span.

Success is recalled unto senility, whereas failure hides in shadowed corners of memory. How about the days when 'doodles were all over the back forty and we missed so many that the dog began to cut a white eye back and wonder what the hell goes on? Good dogs are almost human; they get critical and practically sneer when bird after bird escapes a bombardment.

I hereby invent a basic rule: bad mornings always escalate into worse days. Somehow, missing early flushes seems to trigger a rash of poor shooting. Complaints about sun slant and clutching cover, fractious dogs and lousy reloads never help; cussedness prevails and the world is hostile. It is never funny at the time, but upland gunning would be no joy if every bird was racked down. Underkill whets an appetite. Overkill would be an abomination. That little, wispy voice of reason whispers—*consistency would be nice!*

Whatever the season or terrain, there will be a peak period in which all of the Red Gods smile. In our northland, the leaves spiral down and the hardwoods become skeletal. Suddenly, for an infinitesimal jog of time, the trickle-through is at flood and there is always an exciting possibility of true flight. Now mornings are rimed with frost and afternoons are blessed with comfortable temperatures. The dogs no longer plunge into every woodland stream or pool, and cover turns traitor to the departing 'cock. For a few blissful days, perhaps even a couple of weeks, shooting is superb.

Now the annual migration is well under way, with millions of timber-doodles streaming down the ancient flyways. You catch a few here and there, a minor concentration or even a major flight. They won't lie as tight, and many of them will run ahead of a dog. There'll still be clutching brush to deflect the tubes of a swinging shotgun, but now the game is handicapped—for upland aisles are swiftly assuming that stripped, barren appearance that precedes winter.

We still see longbeaks holding close and fluttering skyward at slow speed, but there are more that flush wild or run ahead before the guns come up. There are the usual complications.

Flight birds feed as they migrate, but often spend daylight hours resting on high ground where there is nothing to eat, but where the brush is both thick or thorny. For good cause, every woodcock hunter's wrists are lacerated and every dog begins to doubt his senses: these strange little poltergeists can and do run. Moreover, as the season advances, a majority of flyers seem to employ afterburners, and their ability to maneuver is accentuated.

The late-season woodcock is faster off a mark than his blood brother of early fall. He comes twittering out just as wildly, but he'll move faster and

Occasionally a cleanly killed woodcock lodges in a fork of brush well above ground. Dean Clark reaches for one of these.

change course more often. The late-season bird is still a relatively slow target, and you can get on quickly and enjoy a lack of screening foliage, but it is unwise to count coup prior to the smoke stream of russet feathers that denotes a direct hit. Timberdoodle, because he is small, promotes an optical illusion: his range is less than it appears.

Beyond fifteen to twenty yards, 'doodles appear to be tiny and impossible to hit, even though they are quite vulnerable to an open-bored shotgun, out to about forty yards. Beyond that, unless a choked tube is used, one gets too much dispersal of pellets to guarantee any effective pattern. Reaching is futile and it isn't very fair.

As foliage thins, 'doodles seem to realize the necessity for a faster take-off and more hipper-dipper flight. Some are immeasurably wild, running ahead of a dog and flushing before the guns come up. Often on second flush they are even spookier, going out like rump-stung snipe. Miniature males are far faster and more maneuverable than hens, corkscrewing through low, bare brush at surprising speed. When this happens I wonder about the idea that a woodcock can't see very well during the day. Nonsense!

Second flush poses problems if only because the bird is unpredictable. One may appear long gone over a hardwood canopy, yet may actually check its flight and come down vertically within less than one hundred yards. Many succeed in doubling back, so that—following a flight line—you find the bird much nearer the first flush point than seems possible.

One thing is almost always true. The second flush will be wilder and more precipitate than the first. Unlike a grouse, which wastes much precious energy in a short flight, timberdoodles seem to gain strength each time they are pushed, and will finally defeat a pursuer by going right over the skyline. Count a second flush probable, but difficult. Don't offer any odds on success with a third.

Doubles are easier on woodcock than, say, on grouse. For all of that, any brace of 'cock is an occasion for figurative dancing in the street. To rack down a pair, both airborne at a single moment in time and space—each zig-zagging off through flickering brush—requires icy skill and quick shooting. Veterans do it regularly, but never frequently. Occasionally, the wielder of a pump or light autoloader will come up with a triple. I have had a share of doubles, but never the hat trick.

This grand little game bird is easily tumbled with a pellet or so, but may be hard to find without the services of a decent retriever. Ordinarily, they don't try to hide, but they are so small and beautifully camouflaged that their location is difficult to find. One sees a telltale puff of downy feathers and a plummeting shape. Mark it well.

Where two men hunt together, another discipline is effective. The gunner remains in place while his partner follows directions guided by the line of sight. This narrows a search area and prevents the frustration generated by miscalculation and doubt.

The best strategy is an almost automatic association with some salient feature of the landscape, such as a leaning birch, the blaze of red maple in an otherwise green expanse—or anything that reliably marks the descent and point of contact. If there is any question, pause long enough to make a reasonable assessment, then blaze a sapling or hang your hat on a twig as a point of reference. Go directly to the spot where all logic indicates a downed bird to be.

Wounded timberdoodles, unlike grouse or pheasants, will not scuttle into cover and hide. Naturally, if they fall into a jungle of laurel or juniper, the little warriors will remain immobile. In more open woodlands a bird is likely to be found strutting like a miniature turkey cock, tail feathers fanned and erect. Those that have been "beaned," or shot through the head, are likely to remain precisely where they have touched down—still alive, but immobile. Strangely, a dog that hates to point a dead woodcock will point these specimens readily.

Very often we make shots that are line-of-sight, and thus are possibles. No haphazard technique is employed. You track a flying bird, lose it momentarily in thick foliage, but snap off a shot because all instinct screams that the aim is true. A good pointer or retriever will quickly prove your success or failure. Lacking a dog, search diligently, if you're convinced that you cannot have missed.

Last year I collected a handsome 'cock, thanks to a hidden colleague. Trudging the swamp edges alone, seeking grouse, I flushed a 'doodle that managed to conceal itself until it was well out, climbing steeply through the yellowing foliage of a huge hickory tree. At that point, while the bird was no more than a fleeting shadow, I snapped off one round. There was no stream of feathers or other indication of a hit, and I was almost forty yards from the point of contact, if any.

A voice from well down in the swamp announced, "You got him!" I hadn't known that another shooter was in the vicinity.

This gentleman had seen the bird coming, had raised his piece—and then lowered it when the 'doodle collapsed at my shot. He showed me precisely where it had fallen, between two great boulders in a jungle of barberries. Without help I'd have chalked that one up as a clean miss.

A confirmed jump shooter on grouse, I change my tune with woodcock. It ought to be against the law to hunt woodcock without a dog—first, because you get too few shots without a feather finder and, second, because it is inescapable that you will lose both dead and wounded longbeaks on a solo jaunt. The little russet feller deserves every courtesy.

Having "reduced a woodcock to possession"—and I love that game-management phrase—there are things to be done. My own tendency is to admire the bird, smooth its feathers, place it in a shooting vest's game pocket, and plan to pluck, dress, and freeze it at day's end. This has worked well for me, but perhaps other methods are more efficient. It is a pretty good idea to tuck a few featherweight plastic bags into a handy pocket, and the trade-named "Baggies" are excellent. Place a just-killed woodcock into one of these containers and it will remain neat and clean. This, incidentally, is almost a must if the shooter wants to keep a prime specimen for the attention of a taxidermist.

If a 'doodle is to be mounted, immediately remove any blood that has smeared the feathers. Use cotton batting soaked in warm water and swab gently—*with* the grain of the feathers. Pat dry with paper toweling or toilet paper, and get that trophy to a taxidermist as quickly as possible. Barring immediate delivery, freeze the bird in a plastic bag. All is lost if spoiling allows feathers to drop.

There are two basic dressing methods. A minority gouge out the breast alone. My birds are plucked, a time-consuming operation, but one I hold worthwhile. The skin preserves the juices and enhances the beauty of a nicely browned woodcock on a smoking platter. All of a timberdoodle is good eating; properly cooked, each morsel is superlative.

Especially when accompanied by a chilled dry wine. Particularly when there's an applewood fire blazing in an open hearth and a couple of weary setters are lying before that fire, twitching in their dreams.

# THE FEATHER FINDERS  7

## Those Necessary Dogs

In the beginning, it was the "cocking spaniel," that miniature, lovable, bug-eyed little workman who, in modern times, too often is line bred into lapdog status and therefore is losing his natural talents.

I have just lost all friends who love cocker spaniels, so I might as well go full bore into the flames and offer a further insult—here defined as the truth that zealots are determined to ignore.

Dogs line bred for bench-show beauty are likely to be worthless under the guns. This is a generalization. Certainly, there are great cocker spaniels still harrying timberdoodles, and a minority of show dogs fare as well in the boondocks as in the fluorescent-lighted rings.

A woodcock hunter must have a dog! I can make a good case for the jump shooting of ruffed grouse, but it would be idiotic to pursue whistle-doodles without canine help. Lacking a capable feather finder, a gunner is reduced to snap shooting at occasional targets of opportunity; he will tramp past ten birds for every one flushed. The jump shooter's handicap is not arguable—it is catastrophic. *You will need a dog.*

Fortunately, our great American timberdoodle is a real patsy for any halfway decent pointer or retriever. Strong scented and usually close lying, the woodcock is the easiest of all upland birds for any breed to work successfully. This, if I must shatter other illusions, is one of the primary reasons for the whistledoodle's burgeoning popularity. A dog that couldn't get within calling-card range of a wild ruffed grouse, one that regularly busts quail—and even flushes phlegmatic game-farm pheasants far ahead of the gun—that dog may do a fair job on woodcock.

Quite naturally, there are degrees of perfection. It is soul satisfying to hunt behind a biddable pointer or setter, one that handles easily in thick cover, quarters professionally, finds birds with clockwork regularity, and is steady to wing and shot. Retrievers—among them the cockers, springers, Labs, and goldens—ensure success when they work in close.

Field trials on woodcock are new and are far from the artificial jousting matches so often practiced with tame pheasants and "Chinese quail" deftly mesmerized and slipped under clumps of dead grass. The 'doodle, with all its inbred reluctance to flush, is still a creature of the wilderness. You won't ride to the hunt in a woodcock covert, and you won't plant pen-raised birds. Therefore, trials will improve bloodlines and champions will exhibit genuine payoff ability rather than show business sophistry.

The first North American Woodcock Championship was held at Springhill, New Brunswick, on October 22, 1972. Only sixteen dogs were entered, evenly divided with eight pointers and eight setters. It is a matter of record that a four-year-old pointer bitch, Venus Warwhoop Lady, owned and handled by Joseph Gardner of Candia, New Hampshire, won major honors, and that another pointer, Shenstone Patty, owned by Jack Mayer, Jr., of Moncton, New Brunswick, was runner-up. The primary difference between this event and set-piece trials on more accommodating birds was nicely summed up by Jerome B. Robinson, Gun Dogs Editor of *Sports Afield*. "To win here, the dog must know how to find and handle wild birds in extremely heavy cover and must simultaneously hunt to the gun without undue yelling or whistling from his handler."

Field-trial folk set much store by big-going dogs, yet this virtue requires some qualification. In this first North American 'doodle trial, judges were just as hard on the putterer as on the unguided missile that ranged beyond sight and hearing. To be effective, the dog must work close enough to be located either by sight or by the sound of a bell. How close is that?

Certainly, it is not the one hundred-yards-plus that may be laudable on open-field quail and pheasant. Fifty yards might be considered maximum, and there are places where fifty *feet* would be better. It's thick in there, and visibility is limited. A pointing dog will always be belled, yet there are many occasions in the puckerbrush when the crackle of understory, the sigh of wind, and a host of other background noises tend to drown that magical tinkle. Who needs a really big-going performer that disappears into the tall timber and must be searched for? This is jackpot country, a place where all the chips are down.

The bell is important. Gunners argue about type—whether tinkly or

Gun-dog setter ready to
go, with a big bell snapped
to her collar.

tonkly, so to speak. Old sleigh bells and cowbells have been pressed into
service; outfitters offer patent models, and all are efficient if loud enough
to be heard at practical ranges. Bell sounds speak a language readily understood by an upland type, and sportsmen with aging ears therefore suffer
a handicap. Hal Lyman tells a delightful story about shooting with an elderly
gentleman who was almost stone deaf and who therefore relied on companions to inform him of a setter's progress. Pushing through a woodcock
covert, he inquired, "Can you hear the bell, Henry?"

"Yes, it's tinkling steadily."

"Good, Henry; he's quartering nicely."

Moments later: "What's the bell doing, Henry?"

"I can't hear it at all."

"Get in there, Henry! He's on point!"

They walked in, flushed a 'doodle, and tumbled it. At command, the
setter raced into a sea of green popples and birch. "What's the bell doing,
Henry?"

"It's loud and clear."

"Good, Henry; he's looking for the dead bird."

Moments later: "What's the bell doing now, Henry?"

"Well, it's tinkling very rapidly."

"Run like hell, Henry! *The dog is eating the bird!*"

Handlers engage in a gentle measure of hokum. Too often they are willing to swear that a specific package of canine flesh and bone is equally adept on quail, pheasant, woodcock, and ruffed grouse. This is patent nonsense. They know it, and they will admit it under the mellowing influence of certain beneficent liquids, or when propaganda falls on the deaf ears of educated equals. We still deal with specialization; if there *were* a decathlon event for sporting dogs, it's likely that some old, flea-bitten genius from the remote uplands would humble most pampered performers.

A famous handler once advised me that *all* of his pointers and setters were equally good on quail, pheasant, woodcock, and grouse. Gradually, we came to know one another and—again—I asked him if he had a true grouse dog.

Carefully peering right and left, in order to ensure secrecy, he hoarsely whispered, "Not one! I sell finished dogs, and it takes four years to break one on grouse. Do you think I'm out of my mind?"

Flat statements are dangerous. Still, there are frighteningly efficient dogs that can handle a wide variety of birds with spectacular success. Some field-trial champions earn laurels in the uplands as well as on a blasted heath where the judges sit astride steeplechasers. Often a genius is the property of a highly intelligent sportsman who has spent years communicating with his feather finder. Even there, the perfect performer is a once-in-a-lifetime treasure. The all-purpose dog is extraordinary—very close to a myth. Yet it exists. *Normally*, we deal in specialization.

There are, as a matter of fact, subtle breakdowns in specialization itself. A superb grouse dog may do poorly on woodcock—and the other way around! They have certain things in common—both must quarter diligently within sight or hearing of a man in command. A woodcock can be crowded —a grouse cannot. Both birds are sought in thick cover, so the true wide ranger may be a liability. No cracker-barrel session ever lacks tales of the long point, in which a staunch dog held until the guns came up—but nobody likes to talk about birds that flushed wild while hunters were searching for a lost pointer, setter, or Brit that had ranged out of sight and hearing.

In the tangled jungle runs where woodcock crouch, a big-going dog often guarantees frustration. Handlers run out of puff blowing whistles, and many return from the wars hoarse from too much shouting. Show me a fine upland covert that does not regularly resound to shouts of "Get in here!" or "Come back!"

Kukonen, who hunts whistledoodles so ferociously that I suspect his own brain is beginning to tilt, offered a guest paragraph after reading the first, rough draft of this manuscript. He said, "Tell them that Paul and I agree on one thing, that either a wife or a dog benefits by a swift kick in the slats!

"Then," he added, "be sure to tell them that you and I are longtime divorcees."

In the interests of accuracy and self-preservation, Paul constantly threatens his dogs with a hoarse "Where's my stick!" but I have yet to see him apply either a stick or the aforementioned kick in the slats. I must admit that we are divorcees, and yet both of us maintain friendly relations with ex-wives.

A great woodcock dog may be any of a variety of breeds. I happen to favor English setters, but maybe that is because I am caught in a web of romantic tradition and delight in their feathery, free-flowing beauty. Some say that a setter requires more time to break than, say, a pointer—and you will remember that the first North American Woodcock Championship Trial was won by a pointer. Flushing dogs, such as the cocker, the springer, the Labrador, and the golden, are natural hunters. In most cases you need only yard break them to take orders, to stay in close, and to retrieve.

In recent years, Brittany spaniels have become premier woodcock hustlers in America, and with good reason: they combine the intense hunting instincts of the true spaniels with a predilection to point. Brits are well suited to rough coverts and are tough enough to take the punishment. Like the fine German short-haired pointer and the wiemaraner, they are stub tailed, a thing that seems to infuriate old classicists.

Don't underestimate either of the popular German dogs. Both are intelligent and efficient, lovable and biddable when well advised. Germans worship order, and these Teutonic hunters are no exception. Show them the way and they'll break their love beads to perform "according to operational plan." Vizlas, originally Hungarian, and also stub tailed, are precise and methodical workers.

Every outdoor writer extols the cocker spaniel, yet few use him in today's uplands. There are probably two reasons for this. First, a cocker is small and is therefore most efficient on timberdoodles alone. A grouse, pheasant, or quail harrier he is not—and this is a major crime in the eyes of the multitudes who still entertain the delusion that a dog can be all-purpose.

Second, from a gunner's point of view, there is a degeneration of the breed—a specialization in bench-show beauty and lapdog sophistication. Throwbacks to the tough little workman of the late 1800s work close, flush 'doodles efficiently, and retrieve gleefully. There are still great cocker spaniels, but you'd best look for hunting bloodlines.

English springer spaniels are larger, tougher, and capable of all-around performance (if not specialization) on a variety of game birds. Like most of the flushing-retrieving breeds, they require a minimum of breaking other than yard training to ensure obedience. The springer is gentle, intelligent, and biddable. He can be a flawless performer on woodcock, both flushing and retrieving—and he will do his best with grouse, pheasant, and quail.

Bruce Woolner, the author's nephew, with the first woodcock of
his career. Cindy, his German shorthair, pays homage.

There are gunners who will work with no other canine companion, yet there seem to be progressively fewer of these fine little perfectionists in the American field. As a sidebar, the male springer is a lover boy. If there is a bitch in heat anywhere in a given township, that's where you'll find your champion.

Labrador retrievers are in vogue. They are big, gentle, astonishingly smart water dogs, intrigued by all game species, obedient to command and therefore capable of working close to the gun in a woodcock covert. An adult Lab can knock a coffee table into the next room with one wag of his tail, but he becomes a canny professional when the sweet scent of any game birds fills his nostrils. Golden retrievers are quite as good, but for some strange reason have not so thoroughly gripped the imagination of the all-around hunter.

Legions of sportsmen go with flusher-retrievers, but true woodcock hunters generally prefer the pointing breeds. There is something both miraculous and mystical about the solid point, a heart-pounding thrill in going in with your gun at port arms. Lots of us lose our composure right there! Nerve ends screwed up to an impossible tension, it is pretty hard to be loose, relaxed, and ready to swing instinctively. Look at any gunner approaching a dog on point. He won't be smiling and nonchalant; indeed, his expression will be that of a gambler shooting for high stakes. All the world seems to hold its breath, waiting for the wild twitter of wings.

Grimly, one scans the openings while moving in. Usually a flushing whistledoodle will search for some patch of open sky in a matrix of heavy second growth, but you can never count on this. Watch the dog! If he's immobile, maybe only cutting an eye back to see that the guns are there, the quarry hasn't moved. Any slight movement of a setter's or pointer's head to right or left indicates that the 'doodle is moving in that direction. Most 'doodles will hold, but an exasperating minority scuttle away like grouse. This leads to a succession of points—and often to a wild flush well ahead of the cautious dog. "Well ahead" can mean no more than fifty feet in thick cover, but that's enough to screen the bird's departure in a jungle.

Among dogs there are minorities of outsiders. Beagles often challenge bona fide bird dogs, and I once owned a dachshund that flushed timber-doodles with pleasing regularity. The major trouble with that little cuss was an aversion to brambles and a slow pace due to his short legs. Border collies, the black-and-white Scottish sheep dogs and cattle wardens, have proved worthy. They are amazingly intelligent and seem capable of almost any task.

Although lots of mongrels turn the trick, only those with intelligence and fine noses really succeed. Bogardus touted the dropper. He said, "The best dogs I have ever had for general sport, take one sort of shooting with another, have been crossbred between the setter and the pointer. For work these beat any purebred dog I ever owned and, I may add, ever saw."

Feather on nose, Sedge, Dean Clark's blond Labrador, offers a woodcock she has retreived.

Are Labrador retrievers lapdogs? This one, owned by Paul Belton, gets special treatment after a good day in the uplands.

This former world's champion wing shot reported that his crossbreeds looked more like pointers than setters, but had better feet and more hair to protect them. "Those which take after the setter have more power than setters, and great bone and substance. Their hair is not as long as the setter's, but it is thicker."

Bogardus qualified his statements by declaring, "Crossbred dogs are seldom good beyond the first cross, although some bred from mine and the Scotch sheepdog have turned out very well."

It is well to remember that choice of dogs was limited in the 1800s. There were the fine little cocker spaniel, the English spaniel, several breeds of setters, and the pointer. Today it is generally accepted that the crossbreed is a poor choice, if only because a gamble is involved. One may be good, though a dozen are impossible, so it's always better to go with the odds and choose a thoroughbred out of dam and sire applauded for work under the guns of October. Admire pedigree, but don't be dazzled by bench-show beauty alone. The name of the game is service, natural skill, and intelligence out in the clean mud of an overgrown back pasture and in the clutching brush where birds are found.

In point of numbers, three breeds now lead all others in woodcock country. They are the English setter, the pointer, and the Brittany spaniel. No order of importance is implied; though the Brit is challenging, Americans probably use more pointers and setters in the uplands than any other dogs. Part of it is tradition, for the two breeds have established themselves as superb workmen. There are endless arguments about debits and credits.

A setter fancier will raise his eyebrows and declare that pointers are too short haired and thin skinned for murderous work in upland briar patches, to which the pointer man replies that setters are just as thin skinned and their long, silky coats soak up water and collect every burr in the woods.

Actually, both rate very high on any totem pole of efficiency. Both exhibit lacerated muzzles and bloody tail tips during a hard autumn campaign. The setter is a burr grabber, but it doesn't take long to rid it of such pests after action. Both breeds are spirited, strong and eager to please; they are America's foremost bird dogs, highly talented and steeped in a rosy glow of traditional excellence. Charges and countercharges levied by partisan enthusiasts add up to ridiculous nit-picking. What'll you have—blondes, brunettes, or maybe redheads?

The Brittany spaniel has reasonably long hair too, and his muzzle gets pretty sore when the cover is thorny. Brits suffer no tail-end trouble, because they have nothing but abbreviated stubs aft. The breed has much to recommend it, including a fierce desire to hunt and much natural ability. Malicious criticism usually boils down to definitions of beauty; some gunners seem to be infuriated by a bird dog with a pink nose and no tail! These incurable romantics neglect to mention the Brit's grand desire to hunt, its keenly honed talents, and its biddable nature in the field.

In any woodcock covert, a dog should be belled. Even where a consummate performer works from fifty feet to fifty yards ahead of the gun, visibility is limited. The bell tells a story; when it stops tinkling, get there fast. Although a timberdoodle may hold for many minutes, it may also sense a confrontation, and flush at any time. This is particularly true of edgy latecomers and flight birds.

Some well-meaning enthusiasts declare that a woodcock never runs. Birds located on moist feeding grounds, especially during the early trickle-through migration, are very likely to hold tight. When southward movement is at its height and birds are concentrated on high, brushy slopes (where they may rest for a day before moving out), lots of them will patter ahead of dog or man. At this time they are alert, fidgety, and may cover as much as fifty yards before twisting into the air. False points are that, only because the bird was there, but has moved. If there is an edging, immediately push a

Hard times for wood-cock coming up: a fine litter of twelve English setters hit the chow line.

flanking gun forward, parallel to the run.

Most retrievers are perfectly willing to locate and fetch a downed wood-cock; most pointing breeds are not. For some curious reason, pointers are entranced by the strong scent of a live timberdoodle, but are disgusted by the aroma of the dead bird. Occasional setters and pointers will actually turn their heads aside in obvious distaste when urged to mouth a fallen prize. A few point dead birds, but more lose all interest after the game has been won. It is not very good sense to insist upon retrieving if your dog hates the business.

Quite a few setters and pointers make one concession. When a stricken 'doodle goes plummeting into cover, they'll find it and make one quick flash point. Nothing thereafter will induce the dog to return. It will be immune to shouts of "dead bird" and be apparently deaf to other commands. *That* bird is written off, so it is necessary to watch closely. Whenever one's suddenly disinterested champion halts for a split second, that's where the dead bird will be.

Curiously, a beaned or head-shot timberdoodle that is still alive but immobilized where it has fallen may rate a solid point. Some dogs will hold staunchly on such a bird.

Why?

Some of the old market hunters had an idea that a woodcock's body odor changed immediately after it had been killed, and this was cited as sufficient reason for a dog's eagerness to point the living timberdoodle and avoid those brought to earth. The theory can be shot full of holes, even though a difference must be apparent. A few otherwise feckless dogs will not only locate a fallen 'doodle but eat it on the spot!

Well-educated flushing breeds work reasonably close to the gun. You see them get interested and practically wriggle with enthusiasm as warm scent increases. At flush, such dogs follow a bird's flight with clinical interest. When it tumbles in a smoke stream of tawny feathers, they're on the way before that inert package ever touches down.

Classic pointing dogs are steady to wing and shot. Yet there is a difference of opinion among upland hunters: some want pointers or setters to break and go immediately after a bird is hit. This is poor field-trial etiquette, but it gets the runners and is favored by a lot of backwoods folk. Much depends on the genius of a dog; great performers will hold if their choke-bored noses indicate another woodcock hidden in the brush. They are frighteningly accurate. If a proven setter or pointer says a bird is there,

Ed Pease of North Brookfield, Massachusetts, and his "kittens," two Brittany spaniels that were pointing and honoring point at five months.

you'd better believe it. To do otherwise is akin to doubting the level steel of a compass placing north in a direction you'd swear was south.

Dogs can be almost human in showing approval or disapproval. A miss is likely to be followed by some ribald comment from a partner. You'll curse a little, wipe the sweat off your brow, and then make the shocking discovery that your dog is practically sneering!

If all has gone well, of course, success is attended by much inward back-slapping and savage joy. One's partner offers congratulations, the dog wags his tail to indicate approval, and you proceed along a run that has become a small slice of paradise. Let's face it, a man relies on his dog—but a working dog also relies on man. Neither is very effective without the other, and each can be disheartened by the other's performance.

All dogs are individuals, and all have character. Some have been known to quit hunting after a succession of abject misses. Others hate to leave a covert, so they continuously false point on the way out. It takes a series of epithets—"Come on, you bum, you know there's nothing there!"—to convince them that the charade is a failure.

A lot of dogs recognize familiar coverts. Sitting on the front seat between a couple of gunners, bumping his nose on the windshield and leaving blobs of moisture, a setter or pointer will be quiet until you swing into a farm lane leading to some well-remembered woodcock or grouse covert. At that moment he'll get nervous, clopping his jaws together and whining eagerly. The best of them know woodcock runs as well as we do, and can spot them at fifty miles per hour on a suburban blacktop road.

Most gun dogs are fiercely attached to their owner and will always bring a bird back to his hand, regardless of who shot it. Occasional geniuses make exceptions. Jerry Kissell and I used to hunt with a borrowed Labrador retriever. The dog had never been broken in the general sense of that word, but she was a natural hunter, and biddable. When Jerry downed a timber-doodle, that tawny prize was delivered to him; when I shot one, the wonderful Lab came to me. That dog was using its head, a thing not unusual in this highly intelligent breed.

All have brains, and use them. Feather finders honor their masters, yet they recognize transient friends in the field, particularly those who are reasonably proficient in tumbling the woodcock they have taken so many pains to point or flush.

Many of the great woodcock dogs evolve; that is, they are broken on other species, with the timberdoodle a sort of second choice. Those weaned on pheasant or quail may do very well on woodcock, because both of these magnificent fliers lie close. A first encounter with ruffed grouse may be catastrophic, but northern grouse and 'doodles are found in the same general coverts, so specialization usually leans to one or the other. A few canny performers are able to handle both, pacing themselves, but the whistledoodle

Paul Kukonen's setter enjoys a compliment, but she's not very interested in a defunct woodcock.

All bird dogs used in w o o d c o c k coverts should be belled. Dean Clark adjusts bell and collar prior to a hunt.

Grouse and woodcock often grace common coverts. Jerry Fiorelli and Dick Woolner admire prizes.

wizard is not necessarily capable of managing pats. By the same token, a fine grouse dog may be a bit too cautious for woodcock.

In the South you have the same problem, though it is less puzzling there because bobwhite quail permit a close approach. It is probably safe to say that a given field dog may approach all-purpose use when tried on pheasant, quail, and woodcock, but will find grouse a new and different quarry. Few great grouse dogs are equally efficient on 'doodles, nor are the best of woodcock feather finders expert on pats. Handlers will disagree, but they strive to sell dogs, and I am a cold observer.

Where woodcock are concerned, there is an initial need for yard training to ensure absolute obedience. In thick cover, one must be in constant contact with one's dog—either through sight or the sound of a bell. Ultrawide-ranging dogs are bad news, and this is true with either the pointing breeds or the flusher-retrievers. If you're a woodcock buff, think about close-range action. The cover will be thick and you'll be pushing through cast-iron brush. You'll have one foot in a hidden seep and another caught in a grapevine. The most insufferable brambles in the world will be tearing at your face and wrists. It'll be hot in there, and you'll get mighty irritated listening for the faint tinkle of a bell on a dog's collar. Thoughts of murder will cross your mind if the dogs insists on going big.

Pointers rank high among great woodcock dogs. This one belongs to game biologist Bill Pollack.

Absolute control is essential. Yard training helps. If a shout, a whistle, or a wave of the hand suffices, you're in business. The electronic shocking collar can do great things, but—improperly used—it can ruin a dog. We still have to learn that dogs, like human beings, are individuals. Some must be handled roughly, but others need gentle persuasion. Count the electric shocking collar a last resort, and use it skillfully or not at all. I hold this to be a tool of the professional and a booby trap in the hands of a well-meaning amateur.

Switching a dog is quite as nonsensical as shocking unless you catch it in the very act of ignoring a command. It is rather useless to belabor an animal after it has forgotten the act; this only fosters cringing timidity. Catch them quick and hit them hard with a folded newspaper or a limber switch. Cuss them out! Dogs may not understand the language, but they sure as hell get the word when you're angry. Just be sure they know what you're angry about! Otherwise, you serve no good ends and confuse the dog. We're supposed to be smarter than they are, but sometimes I wonder.

Start training very early. A pup is never too young to learn, and the best of them absorb training from the moment they're weaned. Great dogs invariably are the companions of men who have spent a lot of time coaching them, working with them, sweating with them. Dogs are pretty smart. One that boasts nose and intelligence can only be ruined by a master who is indecisive and ignorant. There is a beautiful marriage of skills when the two can communicate.

I suppose it is necessary to emphasize again, for those who think that a dog is just a dog, that any canine companion in the uplands becomes more than a working animal. Each is an individual, as full of faults and virtues as any human being. Some are magnificent and others are happy failures. We never forget any of them, either the masters or the bumblers. All are members of the family, and their inevitable passing leaves a void. I know some tough outdoorsmen who have wept bitter tears while burying a grand gun dog, and I count myself a member of that clan. No hunter need apologize for mourning a companion who has shared the immaculate uplands when all of the world was young and woodcock were flighting.

There will be more great days and more wonderful dogs, each an individual. We will go tramping into the green jungles and the sere woodlands until such time as we follow our grand helpmates around the bend.

# THE GUNS OF OCTOBER 8

*Choose Your Weapons*

Quite regularly, while absorbing some ancient account of guns and gunning and wondering whether some old-time scribbler has something worth stealing for presentation to a new audience, I lock into a delicious tidbit. Did you know that the American Indians were rather scornful of shotguns? Having swapped bows and arrows for muskets and rifles, they considered the fowling piece a "squaw gun."

By this reasoning I am a squaw man, because I am very fond of a smoothbore in upland coverts. Now, in the shadow and shine of blazing autumn foliage, I must hit or miss at ridiculously close range—and do so within the time bracket of a few heartbeats after a twisting, twittering flush.

Somebody once said that nobody ruins a shotgun by cutting two inches off the end of its barrel. That homespun philosopher must have been a hunter of woodcock!

In no other upland arena is an open bore more desirable, and rarely is there any need for a choked tube in reserve. We score close or, usually, not at all. Those fleeting mites tumbled at an estimated forty yards are well remembered, and the recollection is forever accompanied by judicious head shaking.

While I was working a New England slope with Paul Kukonen last year, a 'doodle flushed wild in towering oaks just as Lizzie was beginning to make game. I saw the bird away out and high, a tiny silhouette, and snapped off one despairing round as it disappeared.

"Shouldn't have done that," I apologized. "The bird was too far out."

Paul, who was taking motion pictures of the action, agreed, yet he said dryly, "I don't know how you did it, but that woodcock is stone dead."

It was, as Lizzie shortly confirmed. We paced off the distance, and it was slightly under forty yards.

This, and similar experiences in the brushy uplands, convinces me that we can be just as guilty of overestimating as underestimating a killing range. A woodcock is small, hence it swiftly dwindles into the bright blue yonder. Forty yards, by the way, is 120 feet—a right smart poke. Gunners forever boast of fifty- and sixty-yard kills, just as they natter away about the "250-pound buck" that actually scaled 130 pounds field dressed. (A deer always *feels* like 250 pounds after you've packed the critter across a mountain.)

Some time later, having exchanged his camera for a 12-gauge shotgun, I saw Paul make a similar shot. Again, this was a runner that flushed wild— no fault of the astute Lizzie. We were on a steep sidehill clothed with a mixture of birch, poplar, and the nastiest briars this side of Satan's blackberry patch. I was stuck in a juniper jungle on a somewhat higher level, perspiring, wondering whether to remove my boots and shake the pesky quills out, or just quit woodcock hunting, curse God, and die—when Paul yelled, "Bird!"

Rendered immobile, vaguely hoping that the 'doodle would come my way, I had a grandstand view. This longbeak was really moving, not jinking —it was volplaning right down the face of our slope, and I recall thinking that Kukonen couldn't succeed. He touched off a single shot and the bird— which I would have sworn was better than sixty yards out—promptly folded.

We paced it off and it was a good forty yards, no more—but it was a very long shot. Never think of forty yards as close range in a woodcock jungle. Playing the odds, a smart gunner will use a piece designed for fun and games at relative arm's length. At the very least, you'll want a tube that will pattern thirty inches at thirty yards—and that'll be too tight for the average poke. True cylinder is ideal; improved cylinder or "skeet" is fine. Anything tighter is a definite handicap.

Men argue about guns as they do about beauty in various entrancing ladies. Classicists of the uplands decry anything other than a clean-lined, handsome side-by-side, whereas young chargers swear by over-unders, pumps, or autoloaders. All serve a purpose, and it is wise to use that which feels most comfortable in action. Firepower, within reason, is of minor importance; light weight is essential.

Pursuing woodcock, you are going to shoulder through a lot of bogs and thick brush; you will ramble the uplands where birch and popple and briar seem to deny all forward motion. It will be hard work, masqueraded by the name of sport, and you will want a firearm that is both light and easily handled.

I am aware that our grandfathers scored with fowling pieces that weighed eight or ten pounds. Some of the old market hunters actually extolled the advantages of weight, and they were right—for their time. If those excellent upland gunners of the late 1800s were alive today, they'd be just as thoroughly dedicated to the featherweight tool.

There are two things to consider. First, of course, black-powder firearms are antediluvian by today's standards. Although the best were triumphs of gunsmithing, the state of metallurgy then required a measure of bulk to ensure safety. At that time, any big-bore six-pound piece was suspect because it might be dangerous and, in any event, would kick like a bee-stung mule.

Second, the old gunners were tough cookies. Most of them were sinewy and fit, thanks to hard physical labor tilling the soil and caring for livestock. They thought nothing of toting a ten-pound firearm all day, because that was considered normal. Upland hunting was no game for the multitudes; each town boasted a few famous sportsmen who were blessed with muscle and stamina. Then, as now, a select few made history—and they made do with the equipment available.

Light shotguns arrived during those post-Civil War years we now envision as a sort of upland Stone Age. Gradually, with the advent of breech-loaders and smokeless powder, the modern piece evolved. It came slowly, haltingly. Although the classic side-by-side was early, it was nearly eclipsed by Winchester's Model 1897 cornsheller. A few years later, John Browning's autoloader just about buried double guns in America.

All of them in the late 1800s were too heavy. They often featured excessive drop. They were beautifully machined, hand crafted, magnificently finished—and they are now antiques or collector's items. Comparing the great smoothbores of the nineties with the supremely efficient creations of today is like pitting an Orville Wright biplane against a modern jet fighter.

There was a joyous flowering of the side-by-side during the last half of the nineteenth century and the first third of this one when English and American doubles were popular, plentiful, well designed, and available at a reasonable price. There has been no remarkable improvement of this type in forty years, perhaps because a pinnacle had been reached by the thirties, but there has been a wild escalation in price. Today's average upland gunner simply cannot afford a truly superb side-by-side unless he lucks into a beautiful vintage piece for the proverbial song. Today's finest doubles, and the arms companies will hate me for saying so, all cost too much money.

If fired by tradition, you *must* have a classic side-by-side, rest assured that the nonpareils will cost the equivalent of an arm and a leg. There are some challengers made in Europe and Asia at a reasonable price, say under $500, but custom English pieces start at about $1,000 and then the price slants sharply upward. Craftsmanship is costly, and these jewels aren't punched out on assembly lines. Old squint-eyed characters who have spent their lives perfecting an art put them together with loving care.

Excellent vintage doubles are still available, though the supply is limited and prices escalate with each passing year. It is possible to acquire an American Parker, a Fox Sterlingworth, an Ithaca, or Lefever built in the days when perfection was a proud boast and wage scales permitted artful tinkering. English Purdey, Boss, and Greener masterpieces come and go on the used-gun market. Such arms are investments, worth passing down to heirs.

Way back in the early thirties, Tap Tapply purchased a 20-gauge Winchester Model 21 for a grand total of $38.00! Admittedly, it was bargain priced at the time, because some musclehead had decided that double trigger models were phasing out. The Model 21 now reigns supreme as America's finest side-by-side, but is built only to order—and this custom-grade piece starts at $2,500.

A host of relatively inexpensive doubles can be had. Many of them are well built and handle nicely, yet are generally heavier than the ultimate tool and are never as well machined, fitted, and balanced. Having admired a thoroughbred, it is difficult to accept a reasonable facsimile.

But all is not lost! Some of us even feel that the side-by-side is an anachronism, a bow to romantic tradition, and a less efficient piece than its champions declare. There are over-unders and pumps and autoloaders, all featuring single alignment that simplifies shooting and increases accuracy. It is worth pondering the fact that on skeet and trap fields, where powdered clays mean trophies or big purses, nobody uses a side-by-side. At the turn of the century, market hunters went to pump guns, and brigands who slaughtered ducks for the tables of big spenders in the Roaring Twenties favored Browning autoloaders with extended magazine tubes. Admittedly, these were production guns, but note that they were chosen precisely because they were most efficient.

Nobody needs a production gun in today's uplands, but efficiency is still important. The record coldly indicates that single alignment is deadlier than twin side-by-side tubes. No smoothbore is deadlier than the over-under, the pump, or the autoloader, and all of these are available at a reasonable price. Costs will rise, of course, as they have done over the wheeling years. Still, a really fine firearm will always increase in value.

There is one other little nasty fact to consider in this running argu-

The classic side-by-side is favored by a host of upland gunners. This is Dean Clark moving in with a handsome British lightweight.

ment about shotgun types. Some folk simply cannot shoot double alignment, and I am one of them. There is no mental block involved, because I cut milk teeth on side-by-sides and have owned several fine pieces. A few rest in my gun cabinet today, and I love them for their lean, symmetrical profiles, but— with a double—I can't hit a corn-fed game farm pheasant lumbering away like an overloaded helicopter.

You too?

Go to an over-under, a pump, or an autoloader. Critics say that the over-under is "clubby" and a bother, because you have to "break it in half" to extract a spent shell or load a fresh round. Usually, big-bore pumps and auto-loaders are too heavy, but a few of them suffice if you resist a temptation to load five shells. Who needs that many in the uplands?

An over-under is excellent. I have a Browning 20-gauge Lightning that seems to point on command, plus a Beretta BL-4 12-gauge that is equally on the mark when tawny wings flutter. Both are light enough to carry and to swing after long hours in rough cover, and each is bored skeet-and-skeet, near perfection for timberdoodle. Underline the word "light," and insist on open boring. A tight choke has no place in the birch whips and alders.

We now enjoy a proliferation of delightful over-unders. They boast single alignment, yet offer the one inescapable advantage of twin tubes—a choice of boring. This choice may be academic where woodcock are concerned, but it certainly provides an edge for the one-gun shooter who seeks a variety of upland game. It may even help the whistledoodle fancier after frost has stripped the woods and a second long poke becomes feasible.

Pump guns are all-American workhorses. In big-bore there aren't many light enough to carry in the puckerbrush, but you can always go to 20 gauge —in which case a lot of fine cornshellers slim down to less than the critical six and a half pounds. The old Winchester Model 12, perhaps the finest repeating shotgun ever designed, has killed a lot of 'doodles, but in 12 gauge it is too heavy for practical work. A better choice is the Ithaca Model 37. I consider this the second-best big-bore bird shooter in the world—and the first is my own conversion of a firearm that has been discontinued.

In a big-bore over-the-counter shotgun, you can't find anything better than a field-grade Ithaca-37. It is well made and relatively inexpensive, one of the world's finest upland pieces. There are no fancy frills, but you can count on putting shot strings right where they are directed.

A whole host of pumps in the 20-gauge bracket are light enough to carry and are efficient in use. Pumps all kick harder than autoloaders, but a sportsman seldom notices recoil in the field. Finally, the cornsheller is tough and serviceable; malfunctions are rare because the action is all basic mechanics and muscle.

There remains the autoloader, and Americans make the finest repeating shotguns in this world. We can complain about parts stamped out of sardine

The over-under is an excellent choice in today's uplands. Paul
Kukonen's setter is dubious about the scent of that woodcock.

All fine guns. From left to right: over-under, light pump, and autoloader. Jack Woolner, center, demonstrates correct gun carry. Companions Paul Belton and Frank Woolner aren't ready for action.

tins and about haphazard machining, but no quick loaders have ever functioned so well. Europeans and Asians challenge us, but their sporting ordnance remains far inferior to our mass-produced designs.

There has been a strange reluctance to manufacture lightweight big-bore repeating shotguns. That it can be done is accepted, because a few pieces have been demonstrated. There is no roadblock of excessive recoil, since kick can be, and has been, dampened. Evidently the heavy repeater sells, so nobody dares to buck the odds with something light. Exceptions?

Winchester introduced the Model 59 three-shot autoloader in 1959. This piece was far ahead of its time, but it didn't sell—even though weight was held to six and a half pounds in 12 gauge and recoil was largely eliminated. Hidebound gunners scoffed at the "glass barrel," which was actually glass reinforcing over a slim steel tube.

Browning offers a double autoloader, again light enough for upland hunters in 12 gauge, yet we see few of them—perhaps due to that two-shot limitation.

Franchi builds a 12-gauge autoloader that scales six and a half pounds. It's a fine piece, but seems to kick harder than most American types. In some models a raised bead sight is an abomination in the brush.

Armalite has a featherweight 12, possibly a true breakthrough, but distinctive in that it looks like something designed for astronaut protection on Mars. In this case a wedding of steel, anodized aluminum alloy, and hard plastic strays somewhat from the average man's conception of a sporting firearm. Maybe we're wrong.

All of the rest are heavyweights, suitable for upland hunters only in minigauge. The average big-bore American autoloader weighs seven and a half to eight pounds or more, and usually totes a superfluous amount of deadwood and metal. Fore ends are ridiculously beaver-tailed, and stocks are fitted with exaggerated pistol grips graced with hard rubber or plastic caps. A shotgun should be a tool, not a hunk of rococo furniture. One of these days we'll learn that an autoloader doesn't have to be a plumber's nightmare, built like a medium-sized tank, bogged down with pounds of status deadwood and all sorts of little intermeshing mechanisms that chatter and wheeze and require a degree in engineering to field strip.

My own all-around upland gun is a conversion of the aforementioned Winchester Model 59. This piece is no longer manufactured, but a few are available in the used gun marts. Over the counter, back in the early sixties, a Model 59 weighed approximately six and a half pounds and was therefore one of the lightest 12-gauge autoloaders in the world. It was, and is, remarkably simple and basic in design, a straight-blowback type with no sophisticated working parts to create trouble. A spring-loaded operating rod in the stock ensures cycling and absorbs recoil. The gun doesn't kick.

Winchester made about three hundred and fifty thousand 59s before tossing in the towel. "Aside from a few New England grouse hunters and quail shooters in Texas," a Winchester executive told me, "nobody bought the thing." Prospective customers were afraid of that glass covering on a thin steel barrel, and were upset by a piece that is admittedly stock heavy. A manufacturer pleases the multitudes, or goes broke; hence, the Model 59, a really significant breakthrough in repeating firearms, was discontinued. The design will be back, because there is nothing better, and there will be improvements. Admittedly a layman, I have made this piece the deadliest of all upland guns. No sophisticated skills are required.

Intrigued by the gun, I bought one during an Eastern Editors' trap and skeet shoot in 1961, and later acquired another. Some small operations followed. First, I amputated about one-third of the fat beaver-tailed fore end, jettisoned a long lug bolt, got rid of the useless pistol grip, and pared additional ounces off the remaining wood. I cut one barrel back to twenty-three and a half inches for early-season work with straight cylinder, and kept a standard bird-caged choke tube for other labors.

My early woodcock-and-grouse gun weighs precisely five pounds eleven ounces in 12 gauge. It chambers three shells and recoil is mild. The second piece, boasting the factory's original twenty-five-and-one-half-inch interchangeable choke tube, scales six pounds—and is therefore lighter than a majority of miniguns with less clout and more kick. These choppers of mine can handle anything from woodcock to Canada geese, depending on the boring chosen. They are slimmer and trimmer than anything else on the market, and they are the ultimate tools.

All right, it has been said that nobody needs anything more potent than 20 gauge in woodcock cover, and I agree. There are lots of over-unders, pumps, and autoloaders available in minigun weights. Nobody really needs big bore, though it certainly offers insurance. The 20 is wonderful; one may go to 28 gauge without much sacrifice, and, if a man happens to be a superb marksman, the little .410 may enter the lists.

Mark this last carefully—*a superb marksman.* I hold it frivolous, almost criminal, for anyone other than a master of the shotgun to use a .410 on any game in upland cover. There is an unfortunate tendency to consider mini-guns sporting, yet in the hands of a duffer they are maimers or, at best, abject missers. Too many self-appointed experts go to miniguns as status symbols. A handful of specialists are capable, and I do not consider myself worthy. Although I can rack down a better-than-average percentage of flushed game birds, and score well into the twenties at skeet, I still need an edge. Finally, I have been too long in this business to seek medals to bolster my ego.

I hunted in northeastern Maine with a frighteningly efficient bean pole of a man named George Olson, from North Conway, New Hampshire. He happens to be a skeet shark and a very deadly character with any shooting stick. George bagged successive 'doodles with a miniature .410-gauge pump, methodically shouting "Bird Up!" as the quarry flushed, and "Bird down!" immediately after loosing a round.

There are folk like George scattered around the nation's woodcock coverts; they are very accurate and need none of the insurance provided by big bore and wide pattern. Average shooters like me occasionally feel that if George can do it, so can we—and we're wrong. It's better to go with the odds, at least until such time as our skills ensure overwhelming success and a handicap is logical.

The streamlined 20 is ideal: with it you throw a standard, low-based seven-eighths ounce of shot, which is enough. There is no need for magnum loads. This piece can be had in the ideal weight range and, if any smoothbore has ever been designed for the express purpose of woodcock hunting, this would have to be the one.

In northern coverts, the 16 gauge is just about phased out, although it is still popular Down South. I cannot fault a 16. It is a delightful hunk of featherweight ordnance and may sometime return to favor. Where timber-doodles are concerned, there is nothing wrong with 28 gauge, other than a slight handicap when grouse crash the party or when you must buy shells at some corner crossroads general store in the hinterlands. There the 12 and the 20 will be most readily available, and 12 gauge is certain, though 20 may be in short supply.

Regardless of the piece chosen, open boring is a necessity. In woodcock shooting, one desires a maximum killing pattern at twenty to thirty yards, with reasonable clout up to forty, but never beyond that range. This means true cylinder or the nuances offered by improved cylinder or skeet. Variable-choke devices help a one-gun shooter, and the best of them add only a little weight. Indeed, a muzzle-bandage effect may simplify pointing. I have never found this to be so, yet lots of great scatter-gunners are convinced of it. Some, needing no choke attachment, build an eye-catching bandage of plastic electrician's tape at the muzzle. If it helps, use it.

I doubt that I ever see the barrel or bead sight after a bird has flushed. My eyes are wide open, locked on that flying target, and the swing is almost instinctive. I point a gun as I'd point a finger. There is, for a few shaved seconds of delicious time, nothing but a rapidly departing prize which I intend to perforate with a well-directed pattern of small shot. If you desire step-by-step procedures, go elsewhere—I rely on vision and reflexes, both trained by many years on skeet fields and in the uplands.

Sights on a shotgun have always been controversial, and some astonishing range-finder devices, builtin lead gimmicks, and other attachments (including low-powered 'scopes) have been offered. I still don't know whether the single terminal bead is necessary for most people, but I am sure that for me it is not. I just never see bead or barrel in the heat of action. I once tested this on a skeet field. It was an accident, but I'm glad it happened, because now I can bore comrades with the case history.

I'd just completed the customizing of a Winchester Model 59 autoloader and had decided to christen the abbreviated piece with a round of skeet. On Station One, outgoer—the first shot of twenty-five—I managed to powder the clay, but found that an improperly anchored gold bead-sight had popped out to disappear in some short grass. Grimly I thought, *now* we'll see whether a sight makes any difference.

I blew one bird on that round, winding up with 24 × 25—a mite over my head, because I don't average that well with the supremely efficient Remington Model 1100. Loss of a bead sight imposed no handicap, and maybe even kept me from being distracted.

Make of this whatever you will: if I had to live or die with a shotgun on upland game, I'd dispense with sights and stress both light weight and balance. I would choose the gauge and boring most ideally suited to the bird at hand. I would get rid of such unnecessary affectations as pistol grips and beaver-tailed fore ends. I would want all the edges and would scorn tradition. It is human to run with the herd, so we handicap ourselves with little sophistries such as recoil pads. Who needs one of those rubber spronges to catch on a shooting jacket while mounting a gun?

Granted, there is joy in the ownership of a beautiful upland firearm. Many of the old doubles are both efficient and handsome, since they were made for shooters instead of collectors. Too many of the modern smoke-sticks are much better to look at than to swing in a woodcock covert. It is possible to combine lean beauty with efficiency. Indeed, the deadliest of sporting arms have always achieved an aura of romance because they were murderously effective and utterly lacking in idiotic sops to human vanity. The true killer is no armchair adventurer.

Usually, you need no more than two rounds. This is taken for granted with a side-by-side or over-under, and it is fair. Bona fide doubles are frequently possible, but triples are so unusual that they rate as curious upland news items. If a pump or autoloader is used, it is rather silly to load more than three shells; you won't use more, and excess loads only add weight.

This is often forgotten by sportsmen who push a given pump or autoloader as being superior to any double. They cite the empty weight of the piece, but forget that it gets fatter as shells are fed into a long magazine tube. Weight is that which is in your hands at a given time, and the ounces represented by shells that will never be used are sure to slow a swing. It is rather stupid to trim a pump or autoloader to featherweight proportions—and then bog it down with five shells.

Federal law requires that no more than three shells be chambered in any firearm used on migratory game. This regulation is rarely enforced where woodcock are concerned, but it is there. Similarly, although the timber-doodle is listed among migratory game birds, at this writing it is not necessary to hold a federal "duck stamp" to take them. Things may change; there is a good possibility that a federal migratory upland bird hunting stamp may be necessary in the foreseeable future.

"Brush guns" are favored by people who seek timberdoodles. Sometimes we allow imagination to obscure cold fact about gun types. Theoretically, a short barrel facilitates fast handling in close quarters. It does, but another factor immediately enters the equation—as you cut back, the sighting plane is diminished and accuracy suffers. There is a good reason why 26-inch tubes are favored in a side-by-side or over-under. With this barrel length and short breech section, one assures approximately 36 inches from eye to muzzle, and this is a sighting plane deemed most efficient.

Tradition-bound, sportsmen are likely to forget rearrangement of the figures when they are applied to pumps or autoloaders, with their long receivers. If a 36-inch sighting plane is most efficient, the tube can be cut back to a hypothetical 20 or 21 inches. However, because any barrel reduced to less than about 23½ inches introduces very slight deterioration in ballistic performance, that is the logical minimum. A few zealots go to 20 inches, but these tubes are so short that the piece begins to look like a riot gun and handles like a pistol. Such cropping serves no purpose and detracts from efficiency. An adequate sighting plane might be assured in a long-receivered pump or autoloader, but ballistics accuracy begins to fall off as you go below the 23½-inch barrel. Cut it to 18 inches or less and you may get thrown into a federal pokey.

Since ease in handling is important, the overall length of a piece is worth considering. If a 26-inch barrel is favored, then any pump or autoloader will be a much lengthier hunk of ordnance than a side-by-side or over-under. As mentioned before, a repeater's long receiver must be taken into account.

Wealthy sportsmen habitually buy gun after gun, convinced that a new one will cure ills that can only be cured by practice. Certainly, a well-balanced, handsomely assembled piece is better than a cheap gas-pipe special, but there is a healthy middle ground. Field-grade smoothbores produced by all the better American firms are efficient. They are tailored to the average human being, so most of us can adapt. Note that great shooters can chalk up high scores with almost any borrowed stick. Select a shotgun that feels right, and then learn to use it.

You will want something that is light, capable of throwing enough shot to halt a twisting timberdoodle, and familiar enough so that there is no groping for a safety catch. To be successful, you must have a firearm that feels like an extension of your arms, a piece that automatically comes up, ready for action, when wings twitter. There won't be much time to think; it will be reflex action all the way.

A whistledoodle, fairly hit, is easily dumped. A single No. 9 pellet is enough, and 9s have always been favored as the deadliest choice. Some specialists prefer 10s or even 12s, and they are right! On the other hand, since grouse may be found in the same runs with 'doodles, there is often a general compromise on 8s, a shot size considered a bit heavy for woodcock and a mite light for grouse, but one that will kill both in short-range early-season shooting. Actually, 8s are excellent on both birds, and you can anchor a grouse with 9s or 10s. The old market hunters of the nineties preferred small pellets, and they were shooting for cash rather than sport.

You will read some nonsense about 7½s for 'doodles and will meet some joyous warriors who prefer 6s for everything. Walking in to various marshes, I have killed woodcock with charges of high-based 4s, but that proved nothing other than the fact that it can be done. Even with the high-velocity load of 4s, I was handicapped. Because of the size of each pellet, I had less flak on target. A tiny 9 or 10 would have killed as well, and I'd have had more of them to do the job.

Say you shoot 1⅛ ounces of shot, just right in a low-based 12-gauge shell. (There'll be different figures for other gauges, but no change in proportions.) In No. 4 there will be approximately 135 pellets to the ounce, each capable of killing. Go to 9s and you have a wonderful 585 little spheres!

In the 7½ load, an ounce of shot adds up to 350 pellets, still puny compared to the 9. Those of us favoring 8s as a woodcock–grouse compromise enjoy 410 pellets to the ounce, which actually means about 461 in the standard 12-gauge 1⅛-ounce load. With 9s the pellet count rises to approximately 648. Consider the odds—and if you're crafty, seek to improve your chances.

Noting that ranges are short and tiny pellets efficient, some specialists use nothing but 10s and 12s, load their own—with old-fashioned felt and cardboard wads to ensure wider dispersal of the shot string—and swear by open-pipe 12-gauge artillery.

There is both logic and fallacy here. The Nos. 10 and 12 shot sizes are murderously effective on woodcock, but lack necessary clout when a grouse or pheasant crashes the party. Certainly, 12 gauge is the most efficient boring in use today, yet there is no denying the operational excellence of a 20. The amount of flak on target diminishes mathematically as you move down the gauges toward minigun configurations, but—up to a point—the lighter weight and pleasant balance of a little smokestick is an equalizer.

Today's magnificent plastic shot sleeve "tightens" any given choke and makes true cylinder boring practical. Prior to the sleeve, an open pipe guaranteed blown patterns at anything other than minimal range. Therefore, why do some strategists go back to old-fashioned wads in reloading for woodcock? For the simple reason that they *want* a wide, and even blown, pattern at extremely short range! These gamblers feel that a veritable cloud of small shot at fifteen or twenty yards can afford to be erratic and will succeed because there is greater dispersion of pellets. This "spray the landscape" hypothesis is questionable, its benefits usually cancelled out by obvious handicaps.

I advocate 9s for woodcock alone, and ordinary skeet loads are excellent. Where 'doodles and grouse alternate, I prefer 8s, the standard trap load, and I go with low-based shells, plastic sleeves, and cylinder or improved cylinder boring. The combination is mighty efficient. Remember that a shotgun is a close-range weapon; within its limitations it will tame anything from a fast-flying whistledoodle to a Bengal tiger. Ill-used, it can disable its handler or even figure in the horror of manslaughter.

Woodcock hunters are more often exposed to the dreaded 12–20 burst than are other sportsmen. This happens when a live 20-gauge shell is accidentally dropped into the chamber of a 12; it slides into the tube, lodging a few inches below the breech—out of sight. If a 12 is then chambered and fired over this 20-gauge round, a lot of guns blow up. People annually ruin fine pieces in this way, and some lose fingers in the process. Almost always, victims are well-educated enthusiasts who own batteries of expensive smooth-bores and tend to match a specific boring to each discipline. The forgotten 20-gauge round in a shell pocket stocked with 12s is a booby trap waiting to do its evil work in the heat of action. Any gunner who switches from 12 to 20 gauge or—the danger point—from 20 to 12, *must* regularly and religiously check his shell vest prior to any shooting expedition.

One partial safeguard is the use of color. If a 20-gauge shell is yellow paper or plastic, be very sure that 12s are either red or green. There is, however,

no assurance that color keying solves a vexing problem. When birds are flying, we all tend to reload automatically, never glancing at the shell retrieved
from a pocket and slipped into breech or magazine tube. I manage to do it
on the run, and though I have tried to determine the precise moment of reloading it forever escapes me.

A bird flushes. In one swiftly coordinated movement I snap the safety
catch off, mount the piece, fire, and—hopefully—tumble my target. With or
without a dog, it is wise to mark the touchdown point quickly and get there
in the shortest possible time. I do this and, to my own astonishment, find
that sometime between a quick shot and the forward rush to locate a dead
bird or cripple I have both reloaded and set the safety catch.

And I know exactly what you're thinking—that I'm a perfect candidate
for the terrible 12–20 burst. Right—but you are too! We all ensure the health
of gun, fingers, and pride by a careful prehunt examination of shells stored
in vest or coat pockets. That's a critical safety check, and it should be standard operational procedure.

Some friends in the industry chide me for referring to a sporting firearm as a deadly weapon, yet it would be abject stupidity to ignore the danger
of an ill-handled shotgun. At close range this delightful tool can be pretty
sinister. The descending pellets that patter or even sting in a duck marsh
when arriving at 100 yards are something else at a few paces. Within a
dozen feet, any 20-gauge load of low-based 9s will blow a black bear's head
right off its body, and no year ever passes in which some spur-of-the-moment
poacher does not kill a deer with a concentrated charge of dust shot. I'd
rather walk into machine gun fire than challenge a scatter-gun at arm's length
—and I have had occasion to face some very efficient German machine-
gunners in a long ago war.

Logically, one observes safety measures—and demands an equal measure
of respect from shooting companions. No gun should be loaded until a covert
is entered and a hunt is under way. No safety catch should be switched to
the firing position until a bird is actually in the air. No gun should remain
loaded during a noon halt or a powwow with chance acquaintances in the
field. Veterans break a gun or open the action before handing it to a friend
for inspection. To do otherwise is both dangerous and ill-mannered.

Strange things happen. That old bromide that "a gun is always assumed
to be loaded" should be accepted as cold fact. It is a sorrowful breach of etiquette to permit the muzzle of any firearm, loaded or unloaded, to bear on
another human being or a dog. You may know very well that shells have been
extracted, but run a final check prior to stowing any piece in a motor vehicle,
a boat, or an airplane. Be thorough and systematic about this: if lighthearted
companions complain about fussbudgetry, grin and admit it, privately recall-
ing that other men in other days have taken a thing for granted and suffered
accordingly.

A stupid accident can produce many soul-eroding end products: like

Guns should be broken when crossing fences or walls. Jerry Fiorelli and Dick Woolner help one another.

killing a close friend or member of the family, like souring the delights of upland gunning for the remainder of a lifetime, like driving a sensitive sinner into a rubber-lined room.

That's pretty much in order, and I can produce case histories—but I won't. We deal with a wonderful outdoor sport, but one that is unforgiving. There is a rigid discipline with guns, just as there are disciplines in the handling of high-performance airplanes and racing cars and small boats in the sea. We must master all of the magical monsters, else they will certainly conspire to master us.

# UNIFORM OF THE DAY    9

*Dress for an Occasion*

Woodcock hunters are superior human beings. Each is a patron of the fine arts, well read, kind to his children, and adept with a fly rod. He is the type who enjoys dressing for dinner. I tell you this because it is generally true, and is slyly calculated to butter up chance acquaintances who may possess information about great coverts. There may, of course, be a few back-sliding aristocrats who strafe pheasants on the ground, but each one of the clan exhibits the correct uniform in the uplands. There, need dictates a measure of conformity; either gentleman or knave can be mighty uncomfortable in clothing ill-adapted to the haunts of whistledoodles.

This is warm, rough sport, with lots of trudging over muscle-busting sidehills, through swamp edges, and the nastiest low brush ever designed to claw, tear, and otherwise impede the progress of man; it is early-season athletics over soft, warm ground. By the time hard cold freezes potholes, and gunners are beginning to get into reasonable physical condition, woodcock are long gone.

On Opening Day there is a better-than-even chance that temperatures will be right off the clock, winding up to midsummer levels. There'll be a surfeit of foliage, brilliant sunlight, and often lots of water. It will be tempting to wear the very lightest of clothing, including a short-sleeved sport shirt. We've all done it—and have all suffered the consequences.

The trouble with woodcock cover, in any season, is that it is both thick and thorny. Lightweight chinos and cotton sport shirts may be comfortable, but they will not turn dagger-pointed brambles. Unless you're a defeatist, and stick to the edges while a flushing dog goes into successive green hells, you'll be thoroughly lacerated. An upland hunter invariably exhibits scratched wrists, but it is not very pleasant to be scratched all over, from scalp to ankles.

If there is a solution, it lies in garments that are both light and tough. Warmth is of little importance; we need cool armor. Initially this means a long-sleeved shirt and pants that are just hefty enough to turn the worst of briars and thorns. Think light, and think tough. Often the two are incompatible, so a compromise may be in order.

Any shirt tough enough to turn briars will be reasonably heavy. Summer cotton will not do, so you may go to chamois cloth or light woolens like the beautiful Pendletons. L. L. Bean offers a fluorescent "Hunter Orange" model made of rugged Acrilan fabric, and this seems made to order for the bird shooter—it's reasonably cool, porous, and hard woven. Moreover, the color is right.

Wear a tough, light shirt—and resist any temptation to roll the sleeves up. It may be eighty in the shade, but the brambles are always grabbing. Perspiration can be showered off at day's end, but you won't be very happy if your forearms are lacerated and sore. Strangely, a hunter seldom feels the dagger points on contact—there is no sudden onslaught, just a series of pinpricks that finally accumulate to ensure after-action torment. You *did* want to be a woodcock hunter?

Constant fluid motion is necessary in this ring, so shell vests are better than coats. All one really needs is a skeletonized version that features pockets for a sufficient number of shotgun shells, plus a game bag slung aft. The poplin jacket used on a skeet or trap layout can be pressed into service, although its shell pockets are never adequately reinforced and will soon be torn by the cast-iron brush. Even those made of tough canvas deteriorate rapidly, lasting no more than a couple of hard seasons before they are shredded.

There are porous blaze-orange fluorescent jackets on the market; one made by 10-X is superb, though often a bit heavy and warm for those early days when the sun feels like a blowtorch. These fine jackets are best used during the last weeks of a shooting period when temperatures begin to plummet and final flights are moving through.

Coats simply do not work, primarily because they're clumsy and hot. As a matter of fact, the canvas upland shooting coat is phasing out in almost all disciplines other than that of work with waterfowl. Even there, specialists currently go to down-quilted articles topped by a camouflaged wind-resisting parka.

Pants are best chosen with care. Some choose denims, which are reasonably briar resistant, although usually cut tight and so guaranteed to impede the fluid motion that's so necessary in any upland covert. Chinos are comfortable, but hardly suitable in the brush because they are thin. Briars and thorns get through and your legs will be just as thoroughly lacerated as ill-protected forearms. Scratches are inevitable, but they can be avoided up to a point. Some like corduroy breeches, which seem to collect fewer burrs and assorted "pickers" than other materials do. Corduroy is comfortable, and the new breeds whistle less than those I sported as a boy. Nothing is better than specially designed bird-hunting pants, and a poor choice can be catastrophic.

A famous skeet shooter, who was up to that time not a hunting enthusiast, came to share our aboriginal game on a morning in October. The country was gasping under one of those abnormal fall heat waves and he chose to wear light, beautifully tailored flannels. Within approximately two hours those handsome trousers were beyond repair, torn to shreds by malicious briars. The gentleman's eely shanks gleamed in late-morning sunlight and were streaked with ugly red scratches. He made a hasty retreat at noon, after missing a half-dozen sucker shots, and undoubtedly spent the rest of the week applying healing lotions and cursing woodcock.

Practical, lightweight bird-shooting pants are readily available. I buy mine from L. L. Bean, but all of the better outfitters offer much the same thing. Early-season models are made of fine woven cotton, poplin, or so-called "mountain cloth," with facing nylon or heavier cotton reinforcements at strategic points of contact. Few bramble points get through, yet the trousers are reasonably cool. There are lightweight nylon "chaps" made especially for bird hunters, and these can be excellent when worn over any comfortable pair of pants.

Leather- or Naugahyde-faced pants are satisfactory late in a given season, when temperatures wind down, but they're heavier than the all-fabric types, and warmer. Stiff canvas pants are terrible. The "stovepipes" offer protection, but are chafing, uncomfortable, and unnecessary. A man must *walk* in woodcock country, so comfort is essential.

It isn't wise to order stagged models, even though a longer inseam measurement will mean frayed cuffs in short order. High-water pants ride up over boots, and this allows juniper needles, thorns, and assorted woodland debris to filter down into damp socks.

I prefer a belt, even though middle age has pretty much faired my hips into belly and gut. Suspenders are probably a better choice, and the wide fireman's type is most comfortable. Sometimes buttons inside a waistband can be plaguey, because they tend to bite into perspiring flesh. Suspender buttons should be outside. If you don't need them, chop the things off, particularly if they are positioned inside.

Next, boots: I have always been partial to rubber-bottomed pacs, but agree that all-rubber types may be more practical. On reasonably dry ground nothing is more comfortable than light leather with traction soles. Pacs are light and fairly dry, yet there are gunners who find them most uncomfortable. The all-rubber short boot has to be a first choice, *if* you can wear them through a long day. I simply cannot do it—my socks migrate down into uncomfortable damp balls, and I am forever pausing to yank the boots off to make adjustments.

Neither pacs nor all-rubber types offer much in the way of foot support, so the shooter who requires a customized shoe has to select one of the well-built leather models. The market offers a wide variety, and some feel that those with buttonhooks are far superior to the standard lace-up type. I can't see that it makes much difference, although it is certainly easier to shuck a buttonhook model when some spine or thorn becomes bothersome. In any event, the all-leather boot usually is better made and reinforced than rubber or rubber-bottomed pacs.

Don't be conned into buying insulated boots for early-season work: they're heavy and hot, especially when wet. At the other extreme, beware of featherweight footwear; these invite stone bruises and wear so rapidly that they are an economic disaster. I tried lightweights for just a week one fall, and then stored them away for springtime canoeing. My feet are fortunately tough, yet these things offered maybe two points of protection beyond the barefoot boy's summer-hardened sprogs.

There are lots of lightweight types of footwear, usually expensive and not too efficient. If cover is reasonably dry, the United States Army's tropical combat boot, usually called the Viet Nam combat boot, may be a good choice. This footwear is far from waterproof, because it features aeration vents and canvas uppers above leather—but it is light, cool, tough, and equipped with a nonskid corrugated sole. These are available in war surplus shops and are great for dry-land operations. In mild weather, if a hunter accepts wet feet as an occupational hazard, tropical combat boots are wonderful.

Regardless of the footwear selected, be sure to have boots broken in prior to Opening Day. It is both frustrating and humiliating to complete a morning's hunt and find that the afternoon's sport must be cancelled because of blisters on heels. Worse, such blisters take a long time to heal, so you hobble around—bandaged and irritable—and you'll miss sucker shots because you favor one foot and cannot attain swift balance at flush.

There's only one time that I purposely want wet boots, and that is during a short break-in process. Long before any shooting season, it is wise to acquire at least two pairs of suitable pacs or all-leather jobs—and to wear them soaking wet on short conditioning hikes. Initially, this will be uncomfortable, but in warm weather one soon gets used to squishing along until most of the moisture evaporates. By that time the leather will have molded itself to your feet, and the worst is over. Thereafter, anoint boots with saddle soap or neat's-foot oil and wear them religiously on a succession of short training hikes. Only when they are completely "broken" and formed to your hooves will they be ready for labor under the guns.

I stress the need for at least two pairs of boots. If you're a casual hunter, not a charger who spends many days in the uplands, one pair may be enough. Even then, a day will come when brambles finally pierce toes or fray uppers. The chill waters of hidden seeps trickle in and your comfort is destroyed. If it's midseason, there is no time to break new boots properly.

Experience, painfully acquired, dictates backup footwear. The moment pacs or all-leather types show wear, order a replacement, so that there will always be at least two well-broken serviceable pairs ready to go. On anything other than a very short sortie on home grounds, I stow extra boots in a "war bag." One's spirits are lifted at lunchtime, after a wet morning's expedition, by the simple expedient of changing shoes and socks.

Proper size is, of course, essential; deviations in either direction can be troublesome. My boots are precisely one-half size larger than dress shoes, and that is calculated to make room for cushioning woolen socks. Some wear silk under heavy wool; I prefer light wool under the heavy. Either combination will suffice, depending on a given man's preference. A few otherwise sterling characters are bothered by wool next to the skin. Use your own judgment.

Individual preference also governs boot height. My selection is eight inches in a pac; this height affords small armor against any plunge into a hidden mudhole, yet I can't see that twelve inches offers sufficient additional protection to offset the added weight and constriction around the lower calves. All-rubber boots usually feature twelve- to fourteen-inch height, but they're loose-fitting and comfortable. As mentioned before, if you can wear them in good health, they are best in a damp woodcock covert.

Please bear with me while I tell you how to lace your boots in the morning! I am *not* being facetious: 90 percent of my colleagues spend valuable time tying knots in brambly upland jungles. The simple double knot and loop would seem to be adequate, yet it is forever picked apart by clawing brush. There is a quick-release fastening that is far superior—jam it together once in the morning and it holds all day. At sunset, after action, the knot is easily freed.

First off, use rawhide laces. Nylon, cotton, or assorted others will suffice —but the busy laboratory technicians have yet to find anything better than old-fashioned rawhide for a working bootlace, or, indeed, anything half as good.

Lace each boot to the top eyelets. Then, instead of finishing with a double knot and loop, or passing around the calf a couple of times to knot aft, simply pass the bitter end of each lace back through a top eyelet, constructing a loose loop outside. Bring the bitter end around to pass through

## HOW TO LACE YOUR SHOES IN THE MORNING!

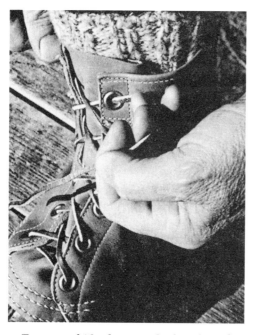

Favor rawhide laces and thread each through eyelets.

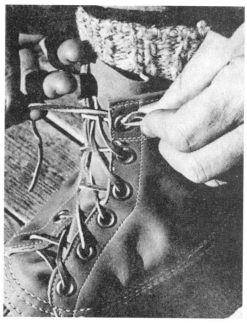

Pass bitter end of lace back through top eyelet, forming a small loop.

Bring the bitter end around and pass it through this loop.

Pull tight and the fastening is secure.

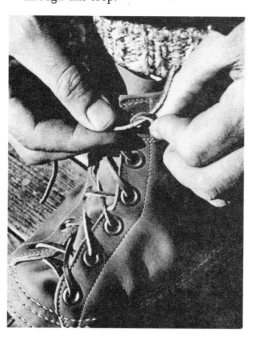

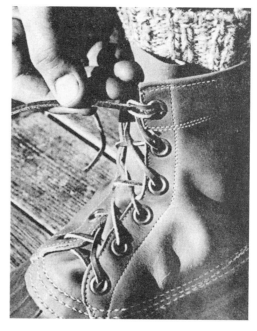

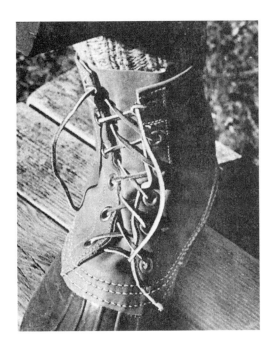

Simple to tie, and just as easy to ' untie, this hitch may have unsightly trailing ends of rawhide—but it will never require attention during the course of a long day in the uplands.

this loop, and draw tight. That's all there is to it: you'll have a fastening that will never—well, almost never—unravel in the bush. There will be two short trailing ends of rawhide, and they pose no problem. Release of the jam is quite as simple as its construction: the trailing end of each lace is simply pulled right or left, and this opens the snugged-up loop.

You'll need a hat, not only to provide an eyeshade with its brim, but also to protect a tender headbone from all sorts of sharp little nasties. The best will be a variation of the time-honored baseball cap, because it features tight fit plus a shading visor. I like the long-beaked swordfisherman's model, yet admit that it is inferior to a more conventional type in porous, fluorescent blaze orange. Stetsons and other wide-brimmed fedoras are almost impossible, since they are constantly snatched off one's noggin by switching brush. Cowboy hats and Australian army issues may be dashing, but they're sorry handicaps in a woodcock covert.

The cap should be light in weight and constructed of a fabric that will breathe. Plastic-faced jobs are an abomination, sweat-inducing and uncomfortable. Forego cute little windows of cooling mesh, sewed-on patches, and assorted club membership or "expert hunter" badges—all are magnets for the snatching brambles. Even without burr grabbers, you'll spend too much time retrieving caps yanked off in normal progress through a woodcock jungle.

Fluorescent blaze orange is the best color because it is unlike anything in nature, glows like a neon light in dim shadow, is the only hue in the world easily picked out by a color-deficient person, and prevents a partner or total stranger from throwing a charge of small shot in the wrong direction. To this add personal satisfaction: it is not only comforting to know the location of a companion, but that knowledge also provides a definite edge. At a glance (often through peripheral vision), you know where you can shoot—and where you can't. This adds birds in a game bag.

Gradually and sensibly, legislators are demanding the use of fluorescent blaze orange clothing in big-game hunting. Where such a law has been passed, sharp decreases in mistaken-for-game and line-of-fire accidents leave no room for argument. There will be a steady gravitation toward mandatory use of the warning color in the hunting of all game other than waterfowl. A healthy percentage of modern upland hunters are already convinced about the worth of fluorescent caps, shirts, and vests—all improve the shooter's success ratio.

Wear shooting glasses. They're a bother, but each human being has two eyes that must, with reasonable care, last a lifetime. Whistledoodle lives in a nightmare of resilient switches armed with short daggers and spears. It is no joke to get "twigged," especially if the twig features thorns. Ordinary conifer needles are fully capable of impairing a man's eyesight, and I am not citing dusty research; my own aging glims bear scar tissue, and it could have been worse.

Wide lenses such as those worn by trap and skeet shooters are probably best. They can be plastic or hardened glass and in whatever color suits a person's psyche. Some gunners find the light yellow favored by a majority of range marksmen uncomfortable in brilliant sunlight, so go to cooler shades of green or gray. Yellow has one important thing going for it: it provides contrast, particularly when the light is poor on a cloudy day. Fortunately, I can wear butter-colored lenses at all times, and I am sure that they help.

Such shooting glasses can be had ground to prescription. I am near-sighted, unusual in middle age, because it usually works the other way around. Fine print is no challenge, but I get a little blurry out beyond twenty yards. Therefore, prescription glasses ensure sharp vision, together with protection and contrast. I can shoot without them, but it would be silly to do so.

Any upland gunner, and a woodcock hunter in particular, is easily identified by livid scratches on hands and wrists during a shooting season. There are ways to escape this punishment, yet I know few timberdoodle fanciers who do so. A shotgun is always a sensitive tool, best handled in bare hands; no matter how thin a pair of gloves, some shade of feeling is lost. The thing is similar to control of a revolving-spool fishing reel; it can be done under wraps, but it is never done so delicately or so well.

Some experts school themselves to operate with gloves that protect both hands and wrists. I think it is an excellent idea—that I will never succeed in learning! To me, gloves are a handicap, no matter how light and pliable. Ruefully, I contemplate jagged streaks of gore at the end of a day in

For best results, wear shooting glasses and keep both eyes wide open. Frank Woolner swings on a departing 'doodle.

thorny cover, and still can't bring myself to wear protective covering on a following day. Tapply swears by golf gloves: they're thin and flexible and you can buy them singly, for a left or right hand. Tap prefers such a covering on his right, or trigger, hand. On the left he wears a heavier glove when the weather clamps down in late October or November.

My brother, Jack—who is a very deadly type in the uplands—feels that the problem is partially solved by wearing a glove on the left hand but none on the right. Others go to European fingerless gloves with bramble-turning wristlets. I just get scratched, and I don't care. These are honorable scars, better than any Prussian saber cut. One always suffers to attain paradise, and millions of woodcock hunters annually shrug off minor lacerations while battling the bushes of October and November. I hold it blood well shed.

Two simple but important tools weigh little and usurp minimal space. Be sure to tote a pocket compass, especially in unfamiliar country—and a topo map. It can be pretty humiliating to get lost in a suburban woodlot, but it happens. Regularly, having escorted a friend into some deliciously birdy tract, I ask him: "Which way to the car?"

Invariably he points in the wrong direction!

A compass, of course, is worthless without orientation—hence the map or a reasonable mental picture of road nets and directions. That grand little United States Geological Survey 1/62,500 topo, readily available at well-stocked sporting goods shops, offers an accurate blueprint of the ground. Woodsmen rely on such maps, and advanced sportsmen always carry them into strange territory.

Compass use and map reading are elementary subjects. There are degrees of skill in interpretation, but no one with basic intelligence can be lost if he uses these tools. Only suckers count on "knowing the country," since fog or a sudden snowfall can blot out familiar landmarks. A veteran never apologizes for coming out "on instruments."

We are an automated people and, almost always, we use motor vehicles as transportation to and from coverts. This is both a blessing and a curse—a blessing because speed saves valuable time, and a debit when any conspicuously parked car betrays a hot corner. I work with a Chevy 4 × 4 Blazer, and it is pure delight to shift into all-wheel-drive and go bumping over farm roads that would be painful for any low-slung master of the blacktop. From late September through December, this machine is well equipped for gunning, fully winterized, and fitted with studded snow treads all around.

There is a plastic and steel gun rack—solely for short hauls—because no firearm is ever left in view when trekking the long miles. Neither is any valuable shotgun left in the car at an overnight motel stop, no matter how

The hands of a woodcock hunter are scratched by thorn and briar.

A topographic map and a compass are prime tools. You won't get lost—and you may find a new hot corner.

well camouflaged and locked in. I have a foam-rubber-padded plywood box sculptured to take a brace of firearms. This thing is tough, it doesn't scream "guns," and it suffices for surface travel or on airlines where all sporting weapons must be declared, inspected, and then consigned to baggage compartments. Shells are stored separately, usually in the so-called "war bag," which is really a plywood chest.

Among other things, there is a food cooler stocked with ice and cold drinks, plus the makings of lunch. Since ice, in our advanced society, seems to be in short supply outside of night clubs and bars, I make my own. It is a simple matter to place two-quart plastic containers of water in a home freezer. Three or four of these blocks in a cooler are good for a couple of days at the least.

Lacking a well-insulated ice-filled cooler, and still desiring a few cool drinks at the end of a long hot afternoon, think about a "space blanket." These ultramodern metalized plastic sheets are touted for warmth, but they preserve chill quite as well. Wrap a space blanket around a six-pack of ale or Coca-Cola and the beverage will remain cool for several hours.

It's your bag of worms, but I like to carry a compact camp stove with a few extra containers of propane gas for fuel. Add a coffee pot, a frying pan, a couple of aluminum stew pots, and basic backwoods tableware. Non-perishables such as coffee, tea, sugar, salt, and canned foodstuffs usurp little space. A meal prepared on a station wagon's tailgate can challenge anything the gourmets extol—and you can add a jolt of Old Fuddlewit if the day is done and there's no more hunting or driving.

The war bag is another thing. It provides insurance, and I have never known a serious upland gunner who failed to tote extra clothing on a long trip. Into this container will go at least one extra pair of boots, pants, a supply of socks both light and heavy; several hunting shirts, and a selection of undergarments. Tote one practical woolen blanket, a couple of towels, and a cake of soap. Cache a first-aid kit for man, plus a tool kit for car and guns. Include such little delights as electrician's plastic tape, plastic bags, a serviceable flashlight, and an extra space blanket. Pack a reserve supply of shotgun shells here, and don't forget such essentials as a backup bell and collar for friend dog. Include a towrope, a good automotive jack, and a shovel. Be prepared.

A war bag should be viewed as a container of emergency equipment. Stock it well, but plan no use! It is there in case things happen, so any item used should be replaced at the first opportunity. Boots, socks, shirts, and pants are prime movers; the rest may be immovable for months. Insurance!

Four-wheel-drive vehicles, like the author's Chevy Blazer, are ideal motor cars for woodcock hunting.

Foam-padded plywood case that totes a brace of customized auto-loaders.

Usually, if you're taking more than one dog, you will want a comfortable, compartmented wire-mesh kennel box, especially if there's a chance of conflict en route. In my case, things usually work out differently. There will be just one pointer or setter, and that privileged character will sit up front between me and my companion, smearing mud on the cushions, daubing the windshield with a cold nose, and almost sharing our conversation with nervous whines and a psychotic clopping of jaws.

Do you find this sort of thing disconcerting?

I love it! It's a nice feeling to have a big, gentle English setter lean against your shoulder as you bump down a narrow tote road with blazing fall foliage on either side—and a woodcock run in the offing.

# SAY GRACE! 10

*Entrees for Gourmets*

Having nattered away at great length on woodcock and woodcock hunting, I think it high time to offer a few recipes for gourmets. There is a stereotyped approach to this sort of thing: one simply researches existing cookbooks and steals that which seems apropos. It is an admirable solution, but one that entails considerable labor on the part of a larcenous writer. I may be accused of many things, but never of a desire to work very hard. Stealing also wars against my New England conscience—unless it is absolutely necessary.

A new and hopefully refreshing course seemed desirable, and I found it through a combination of personal sloth, good friends in the business, and a suspicion that we'd all like to study the recipes of great outdoor writers and grand hunters. Some of these celebrities are true gourmet cooks and some stick with the basics. I am indebted to each and every one—and to their wives.

I contacted people I know and respect, either as magnificent outdoor writers or as gunners, and usually both. Some of them don't even like woodcock on the table, and these have offered camouflaging sauces and medleys. Others grow lyrical, and I will quote them at considerable length because their words are so much better than mine.

Tastes differ, and the timberdoodle is strong medicine: humans either delight in its rich, livery flavor, or eschew it entirely. David Michael Duffey, the dog department editor of *Outdoor Life*, cynically notes that some men "rave about how good they taste, but surreptitiously slip them in the garbage can." He's quite right; there is a status factor involved.

First I talked to Hal Lyman, who sits at a desk directly opposite mine at *Salt Water Sportsman* and peers at me through those half glasses that Boston Brahmins favor. Hal is a marine fisheries authority, but he has hunted a variety of game on most of the world's continents and is a very efficient wing shooter.

Like a Prussian officer giving orders, Hal declared, "You field-dress a woodcock on the spot, discarding all viscera. Place a slice of apple in the body cavity. This keeps the flesh from souring and aids cooling. Later, pluck the bird—but leave that slice of apple alone. Slap two slices of bacon on the breast and broil or bake at 370° F until tender. Split, and serve on toast with port or burgundy."

Harold F. Blaisdell of Pittsford, Vermont, whose book, *The Philosophical Fisherman*, made me envy his skill, goes into greater detail. "My wife salts the cavities and rubs the exteriors with bacon grease. (She prefers this to pinning on strips of bacon.) She puts the birds on their sides under a preheated broiler and broils five minutes on either side. Ten minutes, and they're done exactly to our taste: browned on the outside, but rare inside. I'm sure some would prefer longer timing. Not many would want less.

"For an extraspecial treat, I jam half a dozen birds on the spit of our outside rotisserie and broil over charcoal. Salt and grease as above. Timing depends on several variables, of course. My system is to watch the juices which the broiling elicits and which baste the revolving birds. Eventually, they stop flowing freely and turn to a consistency akin to the solids found in pan gravy made after frying liver. When this happens, the birds are done so far as I am concerned. And, for reasons which I accept, but do not understand, they are out of this world. Of course, the effect is heightened in direct ratio to the blasts of bourbon consumed while tending the broiler!

"I hope you will publicly deplore the skinning of woodcock, for the thin layer of fat, and the oil of the skin, both lost in skinning, help make woodcock the treat they should be. Far from an irksome task, anybody can learn to pluck and clean woodcock at about a three-minute-per-bird rate."

Peggy Bauer, Erwin A. Bauer's erudite wife, offered "Joe's" favorite recipe for 'doodles. She notes a tiny bit of alcoholic beverage, but says it is probably not enough to title the offering "Tipsey-Doodle."

"Rinse the bird well and pat as dry as possible with paper towels. Sprinkle each cavity with salt and a bit of dried tarragon (rubbed between the fingertips first and then into the flesh of the bird) and some finely chopped shallots. Shallots are unknown in this part of the world and, as usual, green onion will do. Drop about a teaspoon of butter into the cavity too.

Woodcock breasts prepared over charcoal provide food fit for the gods at a midday halt in a Louisiana covert. *Photo by Grits Gresham.*

Use the real thing, not margarine. No need to smear it around, as the birds will be sufficiently turned during roasting to do the job.

"While you're doing this, blanch six strips of bacon in simmering water to get rid of the smoky taste, maybe ten minutes. Then pat them dry and cut in half, crosswise. Place two half strips over the breasts and thighs of each 'doodle, and truss the things securely.

"Put the birds on their sides on a rack in a roasting pan. Have the oven at 400° F, and baste the little critters every five to seven minutes with a mixture of melted butter and a bit of cooking oil. (The oil raises the burning temperature of the butter, which may forestall disaster.) Turn them just before each basting.

"They should be done in about a half hour. The sure way to tell is to make a deep puncture with a skewer and note the color of the juices which will run. Rosey isn't quite done enough—a nice yellowish color is what you want. When done, remove truss strings and keep warm in oven with door ajar on a heated platter.

"Pour off all but two tablespoons of fat from the roasting pan. Add one tablespoon of shallots and cook slowly for one minute. Add 1½ cups of brown stock (or canned beef boullion) and ¼ cup of Madeira or port. Scrape up all the crusty bits and cook the whole thing until reduced to about ½ cup. Now remove from heat, add one or two tablespoons of butter, stir —and spoon the sauce over the 'doodles. Serve with mushrooms and a nice red Bordeaux wine. Enjoy!"

Ralf Coykendall, Jr., of Weston, Vermont, offers some recollections and personal preferences. "Three recipes hang in my memories of autumn afternoons, and they follow. One is charcoal-broiled woodcock à la H. P. Sheldon.

"When I first hunted the mythical coverts of Tranquility Township with Sheldon and my father, lunch properly prepared was far more important than hunting, and lunch sometimes consisted of the following fine fare: bourbon, branch water, and broiled woodcock.

"Sheldon was a great host, and he prepared woodcock for his guests in advance. On the day of a shoot he would bring along two split woodcock per person and cook them over a small fire on a rack—basting them *very* often with a sauce made up of one jar of red currant jelly, the juice of one large lemon, one tablespoon dry mustard, salt, and pepper. Sheldon only cooked the birds long enough for him and my father to polish off a couple of bourbons and branch water, which didn't take long at all. I was too young for bourbon then, but I'm not anymore.

"Then there was woodcock à la Pappy Coykendall. Dad liked his woodcock rare and his bourbon strong, and it is not surprising that he liked a mixture of the two.

"Allowing two split woodcock or two pair of woodcock breasts per serving, Dad would melt ¼ pound of butter in a large skillet, add three tablespoons of red currant jelly—which was also allowed to melt—and he would then add one cup of bourbon and bring the mixture to a 'rolling boil.' He would then add the woodcock, cook them three minutes, turn the birds, cook them three minutes more—and quickly serve them on toast with the remaining sauce in the pan as gravy. Some gravy!

"Not to belittle the 'fancy folk' I grew up with, it is my opinion that woodcock breasts wrapped in bacon and broiled (until the bacon is *just* browned), and served on wild rice with a sauce made from equal portions of catsup, sherry, and currant jelly, is hard to beat."

As a footnote to the above, and in the interests of sporting history, Tap Tapply in a personal letter said this, "I ate woodcock prepared by Hal Sheldon. He lit the oven, slid the birds in—and instantly took them out. Blood didn't just follow the knife—it gushed! Hal plucked them, incidentally. We had them for breakfast one morning, which is a helluva poor way to start a day. He never knew I didn't like them, though. He sure *did* know I didn't ask for seconds, however."

Charles N. Elliott of Covington, Georgia, tells how, as a boy, he often lived off the land during a weekend excursion into the nearby wilderness.

"When those migrants came through I could always count on three birds—all I wanted—for a noon meal. I picked them (I think you ruin any game bird when you skin it), dressed them, and built myself a fire out of green hickory sticks that gave off just the right amount of smoke. I impaled my birds on a spit sharpened from a hickory stick and roasted them over my fire until I began to drool and couldn't stand it anymore. I remember those woodcock as a special treat.

"Kayte, my bride of some 30-odd years, cooks woodcock like she cooks quail. In fact, that's the way she gets them—an occasional doodler or so in a mess of quail. As you know, the woodcock is not hard hunted in my part of the country, and just about all are taken incidentally by quail hunters when the bird flushes in front of quail dogs.

"I have an idea that her style of cooking woodcock (and quail) is rather the old-fashioned southern way, but she sure comes up with a tasty toothful. She puts them in a sack with dry flour and shakes the sack until the birds get a liberal dose of the white stuff. Then she puts them in a medium-hot skillet—*medium* is her word, although I'm sure it must be hotter than that—and turns them until they are browned on all sides. She uses two or three tablespoons of vegetable oil, although I'm sure any kind of fattening would do the same job.

"After the birds are a rich brown—unless she gets on the phone and forgets them entirely—she pours off the shortening. Good Lord, it has just occurred to me why our grocery bill is always so high in bird season! And she pours about a third or a half cup of water into the skillet. When it begins to simmer, she turns the burner down to 'simmer' and leaves the birds there until the meat begins to be loose on the bones. I think this takes about an hour and one half, maybe a bit longer.

"The standard southern dish for anything in the fowl line is rice and gravy. With the juices left in the pan, Kayte makes woodcock gravy with a sprinkling of flour and enough sweet milk to keep it from being too thick. Her rice is usually a half-and-half mixture of wild rice and long-grain brown rice (to keep it southern), and over this is spread a portion of gravy. We don't do anything fancy with rice.

"She has one green vegetable dish of asparagus or broccoli, and prefers a tomato aspic salad. When we feel like gourmets, and can afford wine, our choice is one of the pale, dry types like Chablis. Provided there's enough left when we sit down to eat.

"Kayte claims that what she comes out with is 'messy eatin',' but I'm usually willing to forego a bit of tidiness for the results."

Back in Yankee country, William G. Sheldon, probably America's foremost authority on timberdoodles, tells how he cooks the bird.

"I always pluck, put a sliver of apple in the body cavity, inject a little sherry wine, some butter, and place in a covered baking dish. I cook for 15 to 20 minutes in a 500° oven.

"The trail is truly excellent and eaten throughout Europe—often made into a sauce. I don't commonly eat it at home, due to the psychological objection of family and friends. The trail can be cleaned and baked in the body cavity of the bird, but can also be chopped up, cleaned, and made into a tasty sauce to be used as a potato chip dip at hors d'oeuvres time."

George Heinold is an old timberdoodle specialist, and he also feels that the trail is a delicacy, "tasting something like calves' brains." Heinold offers a woodcock casserole.

"Pluck from four to six woodcock, leaving skin intact. Remove the head and wing tips. Clean body cavities with a teaspoon, keeping entrail intact. Wipe cavities dry. Rub cavities with either gin or white rum, and brown each bird carefully in butter. Pour over them one and one-half cups of hot water mixed with one cup of Rhine wine (sherry can be used). Sprinkle with a pinch of thyme and turn into casserole. Cover closely and bake 45 minutes at 400°.

"To create roast breast of woodcock, employ one cup of currant jelly, ¼ cup of lime juice, ½ cup of butter, ½ cup of Rhine or sherry wine, 1 tablespoon dry mustard, 3 tablespoons grated orange peel, and 3 tablespoons grated lemon peel.

"Melt jelly and butter. Add remaining ingredients, except wine, and heat well. Heat wine and blend in at the last. Put meat on mounds of rice. Pour on half the sauce and serve the remainder. (The woodcock is split and, after being rubbed with butter or oil, is broiled in a 350° oven until tender.)"

Heinold adds that woodcock trail is a delicious breakfast dish. "A compact set of entrails is washed in sherry or beer. After being seasoned to taste with salt and pepper, the trail is deep fried in butter and served on toast."

George Bird Evans presents a recipe for woodcock with orange and sherry sauce. Actually, his wife, Kay, should be credited—because she works the magic.

"First, skin the woodcock, discard liver, heart, and all fat (because of pesticide residues). Flatten breasts by removing as much bone as possible from underparts. Keep legs in one piece, attached to lower back. Dust lightly with flour.

"Cook in heavy skillet with tight cover. Brown lightly on both sides in oil or butter. Salt, pour sherry on each piece (about a teaspoon to each breast and leg) and cover, turning heat low. Cook for at least 45 minutes, adding sherry or water enough to make birds moistly brown and tender. Turn occasionally.

"Remove birds to a warm serving dish. Make a pan gravy with frozen orange juice concentrate (2 teaspoons per bird), more sherry, and enough water for a rich brown sauce. Pour over birds."

John Brennan, a nut on muzzle-loaders, but otherwise pretty normal, writes of how it was away back when.

"Going back in history, when I first started bringing home an occasional woodcock, along with grouse, an elderly lady who was born and brought up on a frontier farm in New Brunswick, 'Aunt Annie,' did the cooking for our family. My mother had died when I was thirteen, and 'Aunt Annie' was doing the cooking when I began my bird hunting.

"She used to tell about the men bringing in barrels of geese, wagonloads of ducks, deer aplenty, moose and such. At that time, in New Hampshire and New Brunswick, grouse were not a rarity and the custom was to pull out the breasts and roast them, with plenty of basting. Aunt Annie put any woodcock she might have alongside the grouse—breasts only. She cooked them all together, although I am sure she put the woodcock breasts in after the grouse had a chance to cook a little.

"In fact, she told me that in New Brunswick, in her day, very few hunters bothered to shoot anything so small as a woodcock. Those of us who liked game flavor used to eat the woodcock on the side along with our partridge.

"Now I draw and pluck both grouse and woodcock, as well as I can without losing too much skin. My wife puts them in a roaster stuffed to bulging with dressing—although she lets the grouse cook a while before she puts the woodcock in the pan—and I have no complaints. They go further, and anyone who doesn't like the game flavor of woodcock can eat something else. Personally, I like the undisguised flavor.

"Now that birds don't come home as easy or often as they used to, what with less time to hunt, covers lost to seasonal homes, no-trespassing signs, or just overgrown, we are apt to add a Rock Cornish game hen to the oven, or maybe two, in order to have enough to pass around.

"If you have only one grouse and three woodcock for three people, use two Rock Cornish. Cook them all together and baste with the drippings and you may even convince the eaters that there were three grouse. The basting imparts a light game flavor to the whole meal.

"I might add that we occasionally reserve a woodcock for use in turkey stuffing. We got the idea from a neighborhood doctor who likes a woodcock or a piece of gamey buck venison ground up in his stuffing to give it body."

Recipes that amount to a "wild game cocktail" can be delicious. David Michael Duffey declares, "In all honesty, my interest in woodcock ends right after a dog drops one in my hand. I realize this sounds sacrilegious or something, for I am a serious woodcock hunter and the birds fascinate me. I just don't like to eat them. No bird is ever wasted, because I have friends and neighbors who love 'doodles.

"With that in mind, I give you two ways I've found to eat woodcock and smile. The basic assumption is that woodcock are a bit too rich and strong to be taken straight, but if you cut woodcock with something milder they can add flavor and improve the dish. One way is to use the birds as a garnish for roast beef: In a roaster or pressure cooker, woodcock breast or the whole bird (I skin out breasts and legs) can be placed around the roast with potatoes, carrots, onions and cooked together. Depending on the number of persons to be served, you can use up two, three, or more limits of woodcock and they'll stretch your servings.

"The other way to utilize woodcock is to mix them in with other game birds in a casserole or cream sauce. We often have an assortment to clean out of the freezer. Some, like pheasant and ruffed grouse, are pretty bland. If the birds are cooked, boned, and sliced or diced, this mixture of whatever you have in a rice or noodle casserole, or in a cream sauce to pour over rice or mashed potatoes, is very tasty—and the woodcock provides the tang."

Tap Tapply freely admits that he is no great lover of woodcock on the table, and seems wistfully envious of a strapping son who relishes the birds. Tap's wife, Muriel, is a gourmet chef, and her magic with a sauce transforms 'doodles into a delicacy no human can resist.

Tap skins them out, saving only the breasts—arching his eyebrows at colleagues who advocate plucking and consumption of fatty-tissue skin. "How much DDT have *you* accumulated?" he inquires mildly. The recipe:

"Cut breasts out. Broil 5 minutes and, when they turn golden brown, sprinkle generously with salt and paprika. During this time, prepare a barbecue sauce by mixing ⅛ cup water, 2 teaspoons prepared mustard, 1 teaspoon Worcestershire sauce, and 1 tablespoon butter—enough for about four sets of woodcock breasts.

"Let the mixture warm slowly, not over direct heat, stirring so that all ingredients gently commingle. Continue broiling the breasts for another 5 minutes or more, depending on your liking for rare or well-done meat, and baste every minute or so with the sauce. Slide breasts onto a prewarmed platter and pour remaining sauce drippings over them. This works equally well with ducks, geese, and snipe, and is miraculous if some game flesh is a mite too strong for civilized taste buds."

Bob Elliot of Augusta, Maine, is another who guards against DDT residues by utilizing nothing but the breasts, trimming off all fat and skin, and discarding the heart and liver. Bob vouches for woodcock pie—adapted from a "quail pie" recipe first published in *The Boston Cooking-School Cookbook* by Fannie Merritt Farmer. Ingredients:

| | |
|---|---|
| 6 woodcock breasts | stalk of celery |
| salt and pepper | 2 slices onion |
| flour | sprig parsley |
| butter, to suit | bit of bay leaf |
| 6 slices carrot | ¼ teaspoon peppercorns |

Season breasts with salt and pepper, dredge with flour, and sauté in butter. To butter in the pan, add vegetables and peppercorns and cook 5 minutes. Separate breasts of birds into pieces, cover with cold water, add vegetables, and cook slowly one hour. Drain stock from vegetables and thicken with flour diluted with enough cold water to pour easily. Season with salt, pepper, and lemon juice or sherry. If not rich enough, add more butter. Allow one bird to each individual dish, sauce to make sufficiently moist, and cover with plain or puff paste, in which make incisions. Bake like chicken pie, 10 minutes in hot oven (450°), or until crust is well risen and slightly browned; then reduce heat to moderate (350°) and finish baking. Serve white wine with the pies."

Gene Letourneau of Waterville, Maine, gives all the credit for culinary genius to his wife. He writes, "While quite a few gourmets want their game dripping blood, somehow I could never go for that . . . and I have yet to find a piece of fowl tender when cooked a few minutes. My wife, Lou, I feel, is one of the best cooks around, and here's her technique.

"For baking: Stuff with bread crumbs, whipped egg, chopped apples, celery, and onion. Cover with sliced oranges or orange marmalade. Cook in a 350° oven for one hour.

"In a covered iron skillet: Fry salt pork strips until crisp, and remove from skillet. Sauté woodcock in pork fat and then remove excessive fat. Add chopped celery and onions and a good Burgundy wine. Cook slowly over low heat, basting occasionally, for at least one hour, and preferably for one and one-half hours.

"Seasoning, Lou believes as I do, should be by the individual partaker, since the adding of salt, pepper, or any other strong seasoning deters from the good taste of wild birds or waterfowl."

Charles F. Waterman also passes all laurels to his wife, Debie. "This is the way she fixes quail and the few woodcock she's cooked.

"After cleaning, place *breast down* in a roasting pan. For four birds, add salt, pepper, and a cup of sweet pickle juice, plus a small diced onion. Add spices such as garlic or rosemary. Cover; bake between 250° and 275° for two hours or more. (Young birds require less.) Reheat if done too early for serving. Add cooking wine during last hour of cooking, if desired."

Bob Etsell, a professional dog handler who resides in West Bridgewater, Massachusetts, smacks his lips over sour cream woodcock, prepared this way:

"Skin eight birds and pressure-cook for 15 minutes in dry wine, preferably Chablis. Add a little bit of garlic to the wine, plus salt and pepper. When the flesh begins to fall away, debone. Add a quart of sour cream, chopped fresh mushrooms, and parboiled green peppers. When this turns golden brown, it's ready. Serve on a bed of wild rice. Precede with a green salad and have a slightly chilled bottle of dry wine at your elbow."

Obviously, woodcock hunters are strong individuals, rarely loath to express personal convictions. Gene Hill of *Sports Afield* declares, "Only a brittle and shallow poseur would attempt to do more to a woodcock than barely cook it. Apples, sauces, and other fey garnishes are akin to adding ginger ale to Scotch because you like ginger ale and not Scotch.

"In sum, there should be no such things as woodcock recipes. Woodcock are simply broiled, pan or oven, and served in great numbers with plenty of good Burgundy or claret."

In all fairness, Gene says he is a woodcock gourmand, not a gourmet. "I swear it's one of the finest eating birds, and in order to get my share I have to hide them from my wife and children. Not too long ago I put nine of them, split and covered with thick pieces of bacon, under the broiler until they were just pink. As an accompaniment to the feast I made some toast and opened a bottle of St. Emilion."

A. J. McClane is sure to take mild exception to Gene Hill's scorn of "fey garnishes." Al, one of the world's great anglers and outdoor writers, is equally famed as a chronicler of gourmet cooking.

"My favorite recipe for woodcock is an original, and I have prepared it for as many as a dozen shooters at Leen's Lodge in Maine without drawing fire. This is also good for the very similar snipe. I rate snipe and woodcock even when it comes to eating—both great. And, P.S.—the trail is excellent!

"Woodcock in black cherries:

| | |
|---|---|
| 4 woodcock | ¼ pound sweet butter |
| salt and pepper | 2 shallots, finely chopped |
| ¾ cup browned bread crumbs | 1 stalk celery, including greens, |
| 1½ cups preserved black cherries | minced |
| (reserve juice) | ½ teaspoon tarragon, dried |
| 1 ounce Cognac | ¼ teaspoon chervil, dried |
| 1 cup heavy cream | 8 sprigs celery |
| 2 cups dry white wine | |

"1. The woodcock should be dry-plucked and drawn by making a small cut above the vent and removing the viscera through this opening. Wipe the stomach cavity out with a dry cloth—do *not* wash or soak in water. Dice hearts and livers, and reserve.

"2. Rub woodcock inside and out with salt and pepper. Place bread crumbs in a mixing bowl with ½ cup of cherries quartered, and the Cognac. Stir gently until thoroughly mixed. Stir in 2 tablespoons of the cream and 2 tablespoons of the white wine. This mixture should be of the proper consistency for dressing. Stuff the four woodcock and sew carefully.

"3. Melt the butter in a small saucepan.

"4. In a second saucepan, pour the remaining wine, add the minced shallots, minced celery, tarragon, chervil, and the reserved hearts and livers. Simmer gently for a half hour, strain, and put liquor aside. You may have to go back to the wine bottle, as heat reduction is a variable, but initially 2 cups (minus the 2 tablespoons) will get the 'essence.'

"5. Roll the woodcock in the melted butter until thoroughly coated. Place them in a shallow roasting pan or ovenproof casserole dish. Preheat oven to 400° F and cook birds for 5 minutes. After 5 minutes, reduce heat to 300° and baste alternately with herb wine and melted butter. When this is used up, pour reserved cherry juice over the birds. The birds should be cooked in 25 minutes at the 300° temperature. Check, and allow another 5 minutes if they are not tender.

"6. Remove birds to a platter and keep warm.

"7. Place the roasting pan over a low flame and add the cream; stir and scrape until thick gravy is formed. Pour the gravy over the birds and circle the remaining cherries around each bird. Serves two."

Away down in Louisiana, Grits Gresham is a lover of woodcock prepared Cajun style. Grits calls this "Woodcock à la Natchitoches," and adds that it works quite as well with doves.

"Use breasts only, saving the remaining portions for sauce piquante or gumbo. Place the breasts on skewers, separating each with several squares of bacon which will serve to marinate and also provide tidbits almost equal to the main course. Cook the 'doodles over a charcoal fire, preferably enclosed, but not necessarily so, basting frequently with a sauce made from butter, lemon, salt, and pepper. Turn the birds frequently and devour when cooked to taste. This is a unique method, peculiar, insofar as I know, to Natchitoches. It is a culinary technique that takes a superb bit of table fare and lifts it out of the excellent to whatever lies above. Only a few people deserve anything this good."

Lord, what mouth-watering recipes! Far from being a gourmet cook, my own favorite preparation is somewhat akin to John Brennan's medley. Almost always I cook grouse and woodcock together. Here, then, for what it is worth, the Woolner approach.

Pluck each game bird. Wash the bird in water only if it's riddled, otherwise wipe body cavities dry with paper toweling. Excessive washing or soaking detracts from flavor. Figure one grouse plus one woodcock for each serving.

Prepare a wet dressing built from crumbled toast, parboiled potato, chopped onion, whipped eggs, diced hearts, and livers. Apple and celery can also be used. Stir in melted butter, figuring at least ⅛ pound for each of the larger birds. Spice with Bell's Seasoning and, if additional bulk seems logical, use a minimum amount of any good poultry dressing. Keep it wet!

Because grouse will take longer to cook, yet both birds grace a common pan, stuff all of them with this wet dressing, but see that the woodcock are entirely bedded and covered. Wrap in aluminum foil and bake at no more than 300° F for 2 to 2½ hours. The wet dressing and confining foil pressure-cook and tenderize the birds.

Complete the job by removing topside foil at the end of the cooking period. Scrape dressing off the bedded woodcock and brown both birds under a broiler for two or three minutes. With any kind of luck you'll have a meal that is both tasty and tender. Serve with a green salad, the vegetables of your choice, and always a dash of lightly sweetened cranberry sauce—whole berry, not jelly. With this, I favor a slightly chilled Chablis.

If diners at my table don't devour every scrap of woodcock, I am elated. In no way is it possible for me to sleep without first reading from a good book. It's awfully nice to lie there in bed, propped up by a couple of pillows, feasting like a Roman potentate while muscles relax after a vigorous day in the uplands. Good literature and cold woodcock! When the lights are switched off at 2:00 or 3:00 A.M., I drift into deep, untroubled sleep, lulled by visions of timberdoodles climbing through the popples, whistling out of birch whips, pursuing their strange and whimsical migrations under a hunter's moon.

I have sought them without malice in spring and summer. I have harvested just enough to satisfy ancient hunting instincts and to grace a table. Direct hits will be recalled forever, and misses conveniently forgotten.

How delightful to be luxuriously weary, well fed, eager to sink into a beneficent oblivion while optimistically convinced that this wonder will be repeated time and again as whistledoodles migrate down out of a cold northland. Statistics prove otherwise, but I expect great flights on every blue and gold day. The dogs will be flawless and the guns accurate.

If a book drops on the counterpane and my reading light remains blazing for no good reason until dawn, it doesn't matter. A woodcock hunter dabbles in magic: he lives well and he sleeps well.

*Philohela minor* is good medicine.

# TOMORROW AND TOMORROW 11

## *We Probe the Future*

Game management technicians of this era have a pretty good track record, possibly because they make few flat statements about anything. Professionals are picky about a choice of words. Nuances of expression mean much to them; it is either accurate, or it is misleading. If there is reasonable cause to doubt a statement, then it should be qualified, labeled personal opinion, or not made at all. This is only fair.

I recently asked Bill Pollack whether his latter-day studies had turned up any new information.

"Sure," he said. Then, as I held my breath and waited for a revelation, he said, "It is definite that a scarcity of ruffed grouse has made woodcock the most important upland game bird in the Northeast!"

Facetious, but there is a measure of truth spoken in jest. Grouse are still holding their own, but timberdoodles are more plentiful, easier for a dog to anchor, and no impossible target when the cover is relatively open. Whether longbeaks are "the most important game bird in the Northeast" is arguable. Many would opt for the ring necked pheasant, which is sometimes wild but is more often reared in state game farms and stocked to the gun. You can't do that with 'doodles; or, better stated, maybe you could—but there is no need.

Whistledoodle has been with us for a million years. He has suffered ice ages and drought and the clearing of land—yet he has endured. He was nearly shuttled into limbo by spring and summer shooting in the late eighteenth and the entire nineteenth century. In the life-span of twentieth-century man, timberdoodles have been subjected to various deadly chlorinated hydrocarbons called pesticides.

But *Philohela minor* hangs in there. In fact, there is good reason to believe that "the little russet feller" is making a determined comeback. Nothing —not the clearing of lands, the guns of sportsmen, or the killing pesticides— has entered him on the lists of endangered species. He is prospering, still trading up and down the old flyways in spring and fall. He is one of eastern America's greatest game birds, and his human enemies during the short couple of months of the harvest season are his greatest friends through the rest of the wheeling year.

In this case we seem to have checked our depredation in good time. At the turn of this century protective laws were passed, and by 1920 the federal government had moved to prevent any shooting other than in the fall. Massive market gunning ended before that time, and bag limits were lowered. Almost immediately, there was an upsurge in bird populations. Nobody will again see the concentrations of 'doodles commonly reported in 1830, but that is not a thing to lay at the door of hunters. Land-use wars against all native game species, and the woodcock cannot entirely escape so-called progress and development. Nobody turns the clock back.

Fortunately, our timberdoodle seems reasonably resistant to murderous pesticides. Although *Philohela* feeds on earthworms, which are great concentrators of chlorinated hydrocarbons, the poisons have so far appeared to work no ill on a continental scale. Heptachlor and dieldrin are far deadlier than DDT, and these are most often ingested on southern wintering grounds. Dieldrin is most lethal, with heptachlor next. DDT, though accumulative in fatty tissue, has never been proved a killer, except when fed to captive birds on starvation rations.

Hysterical pushing of panic buttons has on occasion worried gourmets who delight in dining on woodcock. The fact is that no human being has even sickened after eating the flesh of this bird. We don't know whether accumulations of DDT may preview future ills, but Harvard University's computors recently found precisely two fatalities attributed to the chemical, and in both cases the victims, for some incomprehensible reason, spooned DDT into their gullets like ice cream. They weren't woodcock hunters—and shooters need not worry about this particular chlorinated hydrocarbon locked into the tissues of their chosen game. This is no attempt to scoff at savants who feel that accumulated amounts of the poison may cause future ills. If they're right, we'll all eat ourselves into the narrow house, for identical chlorinated hydrocarbons are stuck into the porterhouse steaks, lamb chops, and chickens sold in supermarkets.

So far, there is no evidence of any failure in brooding birds, a thing tied to pesticides in the case of eagles, ospreys, and other endangered birds. That it may happen is possible, but the woodcock still remains one of the most successful of progenitors. Barring predation or abnormal weather conditions, the bird usually rears its average of four chicks. Bill Pollack has found no hint of eggshell deterioration, and he doubts that pesticides pose a serious threat to the species, at least on a nationwide level.

Throughout the range of the whistledoodle, dedicated game biologists are studying the droll little longbeak and banding ever-increasing numbers. Hunters contribute by sending wing samples to state and federal research centers. The work is slow and sometimes exasperating, because band return is meager. Financing is difficult, so a few tireless workers in state universities, divisions of fisheries and game, and the United States Fish & Wildlife Service plug away at a task that slowly lets light into a swamp of ignorance.

Few upland gunners can boast of shooting a banded bird. I have never done so, nor have I seen one recovered. Pollack, who has gunned 'doodles from the Maritimes to the Deep South, has yet to bag one with a ring. There is a simple explanation. The total number of woodcock banded to date does not equal the number of waterfowl banded in a single year!

In order to achieve satisfactory results, this effort must be stepped up, and to do so requires financing. There is almost no doubt that this will be accomplished by the establishment of a United States migratory upland bird stamp similar to the duck stamp. This will provide funds for the researching and management of woodcock, doves, rails, gallinules, and other travelers.

Pollack emphasizes the difficulty of banding. "The name of the game," he declares, "is effort! Mist netting, trapping, and the location of chicks takes time. You may band two in a night, or get lucky and collect five or six. Any operation must be directed and executed by professionals. It is a difficult and a time consuming project, therefore it is expensive."

We are currently moving into an age of sophisticated electronic surveillance. In the state of Maine and elsewhere, miniature transistorized "radios" have been strapped to the backs of timberdoodles so that eavesdropping technicians can tell precisely what the birds are doing at any hour of the day or night, where they are, and whether they are feeding, loafing, or roosting. The "beep" in an earphone adds a new dimension and ensures a proliferation of knowledge.

Most of the erudite folk who are intrigued by woodcock forget office hours and contribute lots of unpaid overtime. The best of them are upland gunners in the proper season, so they own efficient pointing dogs to aid in locating nests and immature birds. Pollack has had a succession of great pointers, and the State of Massachusetts does not pay for spectacular bloodlines, yard breaking, and the immense amount of work that goes into the finishing of a magnificent feather finder. Zealous researchers contribute much sweat and cash to advance knowledge. Even then, they often suffer harassment by bureaucracy and an ill-informed citizenry.

We are *not* on the brink of disaster. Indeed, if world citizens are wise, we may even have reached a turning point, beyond which is a good and logical management of the ecosystem. If there is a true Silent Spring, it will be achieved only through population explosion and abject mismanagement as metropolis mushrooms.

Woodcock are now abundant! There is a good possibility that they are more plentiful than any other game species, possibly excepting the dove, along all flyways east of the Mississippi River. Annual trickle-through and flight produces more upland targets than all of the naturally propagated grouse and game-farm pheasants combined. Few flyers offer so great a challenge, yet in many areas the longbeak is underharvested.

Bill Pollack's wry observation that woodcock prosper as game birds when grouse are "down" is true. The great thing about 'doodles is that they are there, holding their own, possibly adding to their numbers with each passing year. Present seasonal gunning frameworks and bag limits pose no threat. Whistledoodles may decline, but not because hunters harvest a renewable resource; their share will be ever lighter as the mass diminishes.

As we move toward the end of this century and enter a new age, there will be more building "development" in wetlands, more metropolises, and a predictable lessening of wild lands. Every hamlet strives to become a city, even though its inhabitants settled there for rural delights. Farms are ruthlessly phased out by excessive taxes. Greenbelts are plundered. Pretty soon the old coverts are gone and it is necessary to travel much farther into the hinterland in order to flush a grouse or a woodcock.

Ironically, as so-called progress triumphs, the wild and wonderful American heritage recedes into history. We see a strange conflict between well-meaning empire builders who profess a great love for the sylvan environment all the while they destroy it with drainage, cement, and steel.

There are in many states laws against picking certain wild flowers, but there is no law against bulldozing an entire hillside where these blooms proliferate. In other words, it is a crime to pick a flower, but it is perfectly legal to destroy one hundred acres of them when a tract has been given over to the hungry developers.

It would be overreacting to protest all development, yet there is a case for intelligent appraisal and a dismissal of the double standard. Wise legislators have posted short gunning seasons and safe bag limits on game birds and mammals. Do-gooders protest even this, but are strangely silent when industry or development destroys thousands of acres, thus killing resident populations of wildlife and denying, forever, any return of them.

If you're a cynic, the law seems to declare that biological ecosystems must be maintained—*unless* the destroyer files a plan that documents the proportion of destruction and promises to make amends. Having prepared such a blueprint, the developer may then tear the living earth apart, divert its streams, drain its wetlands, fill swamps, and kill all flora and fauna thereon. The paranoid assumption is that nature will not be affected, even though gravel, tarmac, cement, and steel replace peat bogs and alders.

Those of us now living who love woodcock will not be affected. Extermination will not occur in our lifetime, if only because the North American continent is vast and it will take a lot of time to fill every swamp and dam up every seep. But tomorrow's children may be less fortunate if the trend continues. Wetlands are not indestructible and, when they go, there will be problems that have nothing to do with the woodcock that shall long have disappeared.

Our progress, unless it is checked in time, guarantees slow suicide for humanity—and the future of woodcock is therefore immaterial. Indeed, the steady attrition levied on all living things of woods and fields and waters presages self-destruction. Only an ornithologist or an upland hunter thinks about timberdoodles, but the birdman is quite as important as any diplomat; his narrow field of interest charts a possible crash dive to chaos. The slightest dislocation of any natural cog in the ecosystem affects other forces. If the stinging no-see-um is wiped off the face of this earth as a species, then there must be reorganization of the biological ecosystem. We can meddle too much.

That we have done so in the past is readily apparent. There are species that have been wiped off the earth by man, and, make no mistake, man is the ultimate predator—the deadliest of killers. Our major error lies in assuming that hunters have always been ultimate destroyers. The exact opposite is true.

There is absolutely no instance of hunters destroying a species! Extermination has always been accomplished by land use, by calculated destruction as in the case of the American bison to starve hostile Indians (fortunately never pursued to a "final solution"), by the introduction of dangerous and exotic foreign species, by imported diseases, and by the simple expedient of transforming a fruitful land into a biological desert. Hunters have been guilty of overharvesting, and so reducing game populations, but to charge them with exterminating a species is akin to the myth that you can destroy a hill of ants by stepping on one insect at a time. It just doesn't work that way.

The man behind a gun has been wildlife's best friend. Sportsmen cough up millions of dollars annually, and these funds are used to ensure that game birds will multiply and game mammals will prosper. Truly endangered species are those that hold no interest for gunners! Nobody subsidizes them, and the wailing of tightwads is a poor substitute for money to fund habitat improvement and management by trained professionals.

Cynically, I hold that the only way to ensure survival of America's majestic symbol, the bald eagle, is to make it a trophy game bird and find some way to convert that grand raptor into a gourmet meal. If this could be done, a few million sportsmen would scream for protection and pour their dollars into intelligent management. They'd not only save the bird, they'd build populations to record levels.

This is no pipe dream, because there are precedents. The wild turkey became an endangered species in America because it was good to eat and because both hunting and land use threatened its existence. When sportsmen found that gobblers were going down the· drain, they simply raised hell! These supposedly hardhearted characters demanded closed seasons and management and restocking where habitat allowed. They poured oodles of shekels into an almost holy crusade—and the turkey came back! Never worry about the wild turkey in today's America: gunners saved that magnificent bird.

Shooters have made mistakes, and have been big enough to admit error—but they leap to the assistance of any endangered species and they plunk down huge sums of money for habitat improvement and management. No intelligent gunner trusts the questionable balance of nature: he looks at the situation and calls in trained game biologists. He wants abundance, so that there can be a renewable harvest. He puts his money where his mouth is. Lots of money.

An easterner, I haven't eaten a bluebird pie in years! Come to think of it, I never heard of anyone shooting a bluebird, yet these cheery little migrants are in short supply. Nobody knows what combination of elemental fury or pesticides led to their decline, but it wasn't the guns.

The guns, I hold, are never a very important factor in the decline of any species. Remember that ant hill? Weather and the march of civilization are killers because they slaughter en masse. The shooter is a piker and a whipping boy.

Woodcock still flutter into New York's Central Park, and some of them are able to lift off and go southward to the relative wilderness of Cape May, New Jersey. More bash their curious little brains out against skyscrapers. Three hundred and fifty years is too short a time to defend against tragedy through any evolutionary process. There will be greater slaughter as the steel and cement arteries of metropolis creep north and south along this flyway. We cannot be optimistic about the distant future.

It will take a long time, say another hundred years at a minimum. America is a vast landmass, and there are always alternative areas while the busy developers fill wetlands and build apartment complexes on ancient singing grounds. Woodcock will twitter down the flyways as long as there are greenbelts where they can refuel and loaf away the sunny afternoons. As long as there are earthworms and little plots of ground where they can parachute in, we will have them with us. The northland is huge; Gulf Coast wintering grounds are equally remote, burgeoning with new industry and housing, yet graced by tremendous areas of wilderness. America remains a sylvan giant, blessed by immaculate wetlands and woodlands and unspoiled wilderness from the southern Canadian bush to the big swamps, the piney woods, and the bayous of the South. We have time, and we must fight a constant delaying action against the big battalions of thoughtless development.

Given half a chance, whistledoodle will survive and prosper. Like the grouse, a woodcock asks nothing of humankind—our grand little longbeak will survive you and me, if only because he is adaptable and prolific. If we play our cards right, he will be around for a long time—a retiring little gnome of the brushy slopes and seeps, a transient delight, a joy on the table. We owe him the respect reserved for a worthy adversary—and the protection that is due any magnificent wild creature of the American wilderness.

There are other arguments to bolster optimism about the future of woodcock and wildlife in general. Rachel Carson, may she be nominated for sainthood, infuriated rapacious chemical manufacturers and alerted a nation. Thanks to Carson alone, the murderous chlorinated hydrocarbons have been brought under a measure of control. Great scientists have said the same thing, but their reports were no more than dusty papers in the libraries of colleagues. Carson took her case to the people and she benefited the whole living world.

Today the human population explosion in America has been contained. Citizens are now demanding greenbelts and wildlife sanctuaries. These may be Audubon inspired or established by a host of other agencies including the various divisions of fisheries and game of local and federal government. Certainly, any acreage put aside for wildlife is valuable, if only because it cannot be gobbled up by developers. At five minutes to twelve we seem to be recognizing a need for the green world, and this is healthy.

Woodcock remain mysterious and little known. Much research is needed to guide sound management, and research is expensive. Cracker-barrel comment from the hinterlands favors use of the federal migratory bird-hunting stamp, levied on timberdoodle addicts. That won't work, because wildfowlers rightly consider their fund inviolate. The answer is a separate migratory *upland* bird hunting stamp, and this is inevitable. Approximately one-third of today's shooters (according to polls) are willing to accept it, and the remainder will grudgingly agree if they think the funds will be put to good use.

I'd guess that there will be a federal stamp within a few years, and though I gag at the prospect of a separate ticket for each species of fish and game, it seems logical to use this approach in order to finance research of the few that are nation spanning and must be studied on an international level. We must pay our way.

There have been declarations that the woodcock is a gentleman's bird, and that a gentleman is defined as a cultured, well-barbered, middle-aged

type who sips bourbon, fishes with a fly, and often feels that the republic went to hell when Franklin Delano Roosevelt emerged like a demon out of the flames. I cannot agree.

I have seen a photograph of Tom Gresham, the son of Louisiana outdoor writer Grits Gresham, edging up on a solid point; and another of my nephew, Bruce Woolner, with the first woodcock he ever brought to account. A few days later Bruce jumped two grouse and bagged both! I advised my brother to keep him out of our better coverts.

Young men come on and they will be far better than we have been. They have better shotguns and ammunition, the finest dogs this world has seen, half a continent to range, and the means to travel. A few of these apprentices are sure to become awesome authorities as they grow older; they will create a new literature and will quote today's chroniclers with a mixture of loving-kindness and disdain. Why not?

It is unthinkable to contemplate a world bereft of woodcock. We need comings and goings in the cold springtime and the hectic flush of fall. I still envision timberdoodles etched against a full moon, even though I know that this is ridiculous—but is there any man of our company who wars against a dream?

Sheldon may chuckle, scanning his statistics, and Pollack is likely to say that I'm a harmless nut in a ragged hunting vest. Lyman likes to natter away about "Woolner's poison corn," and Dr. Leslie Glasgow, away down in Louisiana, may think that I get overenthusiastic. Tapply will just grin, a perfect image of the Cheshire cat. Burt Spiller, rest his immortal soul, is gone. *He'd* agree, because he was an incurable romantic. Jack Knight, also long gone, was a believer. One must not discount romance.

You want to know something? Every man I have named, including those who have hunted around the bend, feels—or felt—that the American woodcock is something very special. I concur with them in making a case for a game bird that is both mysterious and thrilling, all-American, beautiful to behold, deceptive in evasive flight, a treasure to collect and to prepare as a gourmet meal.

Love timberdoodle, but never take him for granted. Count him an easy mark at your peril. Protect him forever. If you want to indulge in nonsense about moonlight and poltergeists and flights that never materialize, that's all right too. I'm a member of the club.

Just keep *Philohela minor* healthy, with us in spring and fall.

The rest of it will fall into line.

# SELECTED BIBLIOGRAPHY

Blaisdell, Harold F. *Hunting Secrets of the Experts*. Edited by Vlad Evanoff. Doubleday, 1964.

Bogardus, Capt. A. W. *Field, Cover and Trap Shooting*. Forest & Stream, 1891.

Bump, Gardiner; Darrow, Robert W.; Edminster, Frank C.; and Crissey, Walter F. *The Ruffed Grouse*, New York State Conservation Department, 1947.

Carson, Rachel. *Silent Spring*. Houghton Mifflin, 1962.

Forester, Frank. *Frank Forester's Field Sports*. Stringer & Townsend, 1848.

———*Frank Forester's American Game*. Orange, Judd & Co., 1873.

Hall, Henry Marion. *Woodcock Ways*. Oxford University Press, 1946.

Hallock, Charles. *The Sportsman's Gazetteer and General Guide. Field & Stream*, 1878.

Heilner, Van Campen. *Our American Game Birds*. Doubleday, 1941.

Heinold, George. *The Love Life of a Shy Bird. Saturday Evening Post*, July 23, 1960.

Knight, John Alden. *Woodcock*. Alfred A. Knopf, 1944.

Krohn, William B. *Banded Maine Woodcock, Maine Fish and Game*, Spring, 1973.

———, with Ray B. Owen, Jr., *Any Woodcock in Your Back Forty Tonight? Maine Fish and Game*, Summer, 1973.

Liscinski, Steve. *The Pennsylvania Woodcock Management Study*. Research Bulletin No. 171. Pennsylvania Game Commission, 1972.

Madson, John. *Ruffed Grouse*. Winchester Press, 1969.

Martin, John Stuart. *The Little Swamp Lover. Yankee Magazine,* October 1970.

Matthiessen, Peter, with Gardner D. Stout, Robert Verity Clem, and Ralph S. Palmer, *The Shorebirds of North America*. Viking Press, 1967.

Mendall, Howard L., and Aldous, Clarence M. *The Ecology and Management of the American Woodcock*. Maine Cooperative Wildlife Research Unit, 1943.

Rich, Walter H. *Feathered Game of the Northeast*. T. Y. Crowell & Co., 1907.

Shapton, Warren. *Sir Jonathan Woodcock. Michigan Conservation*, September–October 1962.

Sheldon, William G. *The Book of the American Woodcock*. University of Massachusetts Press, 1967.

Spiller, Burton L. *Grouse Feathers*. Crown, 1972.

———*More Grouse Feathers*. Crown, 1972.

Tapply, Horace G. *The Sportsman's Notebook*. Holt, Rinehart, 1964.

Thomas, B. *The Shooter's Guide*. Gale and Curtis, 1811.

Waterman, Charles F. *Hunting Upland Birds*. Winchester Press, 1972.

———*Hunting in America*. Holt, Rinehart & Winston, 1973.

———*The Hunter's World*. Ridge Press, 1970.

# INDEX

## A

Albany, New York, 49
Alders, evaluation of, 53
Aldous, Clarence M., xii
Alexander, Pal, 22, 31
Anderson, Bob, 67
Andonian, Bob, 46
Andresen, Spider, 63
Automatic transport, 134, 136
  Kennel boxes, 137

## B

Banding results, 155
Bauer, Erwin A., vii, 140
Bauer, Peggy, 140
Bean, L. L., 126, 127
Beaned birds, 90, 102
Beating of covers, 33, 35
Bells, for dogs, 94, 106
Belton, Paul, 62
Belts and suspenders, 127
Berchulski, Stan, vii
Blaisdell, Harold F., vii, 140
Bogardus, Capt. Adam H., 34, 37, 38,
    76, 99
Book of the American Woodcock,
    The, xiii
Boots, hunting, 127
Brennan, John, vii, 145
Browning firearms, 114

## C

Cape May, New Jersey, 49, 63
Carson, Rachel, 23, 159
Clark, Dean, 84, 89, 102, 105, 112
Clark, John, 29
Clothing and equipment, 125
Coverts, 40, 52, 156
  Prospecting, 69
  Southern, 63
  Types, 53, 55
Coykendall, Pappy, 142
Coykendall, Ralf, vii, 142

## D

Devine, Andy, 64, 68
Dodge, Wendell E., vii
Dog work, 81, 87, 93
Dogs for woodcock, 93
Dover-Foxcroft, Maine, 47
Duffy, David Michael, vii, 140, 146
Dusking, 36, 48

## E

Ecology and Management of the
    American Woodcock, The, xiii
Ego factor, 79

Elliot, Bob, vii, 147
Elliott, Charles N., vii, 143
English woodcock, 1
Etsell, Bob, vii, 148
Evans, George Bird, vii, 65, 145
Evans, Kay, 69

F

*Field, Cover, and Trap Shooting*, 34
*Field Sports in the United States*, 36
Field trials, 94
Fiorelli, Jerry, 61, 106, 124
Firelighting, 33, 35
Flanker strategy, 82
Flight versus trickle-through, 47, 48, 88
Fluorescent clothing, 81, 126, 131

G

Gardner, Joseph, 94
Glasgow, Dr. Leslie, xiii, 63, 161
Gloves, 57, 132
Gresham, Grits, vii, 64, 141, 149
Gresham, Tom, 71, 160
Grouse, comparison, 75, 82, 104, 106
Gun carry, 116
Gun cases, 135, 137
Gun safety, 123
Gunner strategy, 75
Guns, modern, 112
Guns, muzzle loaders, 33, 111

H

Heinold, George, vii, 144
Herbert, William Henry ("Frank Forester"), 34, 36, 38
Hill, Gene, vii, 148
Hobart, Gardner M., 6
Hunt, Lynn Bogue, xii
Hunting, best grounds, 45

Hunting, first records, 33
Hunting hours, 87
Hunting, optimum ranges, 89
Hunting protocol, 81
*Hunting Upland Birds*, 64

I

Igallo, Joe, vii
Ithaca firearms, 37, 114

J

Johnson, Miles L., 37

K

Kissell, Jerry, 55, 104
Knight, Jack, 161
Korenblum, Arnold, vii
Kukonen, Paul, vii, 58, 71, 81, 86, 96, 105, 109

L

Laine, Arnold, 29
Lead, on flying bird, 79
LeJeune, Paul, 33
Letourneau, Gene, vii, 147
Liscinski, Steve, vii, 20
Lyman, Hal, vii, 9, 95, 140, 161
Lyons, Nick, vii

M

McClane, Al, vii, 148
Management and the future, 153
Market hunting, 35
Marsh, Francis II, vii
Marsman, John, 71
Martha's Vineyard, 63
Mating, 32

Mayer, Jack, Jr., 94
Mendall, Howard L., xiii
Migration, 19, 43, 46
Migratory Bird Act of 1918, 36
Mist net, 5
Moon phase, 49, 160

N

Native versus resident birds, 47
Natural predators, 23

O

Olson, George, 118
Orange County, New York, 34

P

Pants, 126
Peabody, George, 38
Pease, Edwin, 87, 103
Pendleton shirts, 126
Penobscot River, Maine, 29
Pesticide danger, 154
Philosophical Fisherman, The, 140
Pollack, E. Michael, vii, 16, 18, 45,
    107, 155, 161
Pope, Alexander, xii
Post-kill tactics, 91

R

Ranges, 110, 119
Remington firearms, 119
Research, 155
Ripley, A. Lassell, xii
Robinson, Jerome B., 94
Rogers, Claude, 65

S

Salt Water Sportsman, 63, 140
Sheldon, H. P., 142
Sheldon, William G., vii, xiii, 5, 6,
    12, 26, 144, 161
Shenstone Patty, 94
Shooting glasses, 132
Shooting vests and coats, 126
Shot sizes and leads, 121
Shot strings, 80
Shotgun sights, 119
Shotguns, 80
Silent Spring, 23
Singing ground, 7, 25, 29
    Combat over, 30
    Display and time element, 26, 28,
        30
    Nesting, in relation to, 30
    Successive use, 30
Skeet and trap, 85
Skylining (See "dusking"), 36
Snap-shooting, 80
Spiller, Burton L., xii, 161
Sports Afield, 94, 148
Springhill, New Brunswick, 94
Summer shooting, 34, 36
Swedberg, Jack, vii

T

Tapply, H. G., vii, 22, 30, 46, 54,
    79, 86, 112, 143, 146, 161
Topographical maps, 133

U

Ultra-violet hypothesis, 9
Upland bird stamp, 159

V

Venus Warwhoop Lady, 94

## W

War bag, 136
Waterman, Charles F., vii, 48, 64, 148
Wet woodlands, 62
Whitney, Charles, 29
Winchester firearms, 12, 39, 112, 114, 116, 117
Wood, C. P., vii, 65, 70
Wood, Dick, vii, 63
Woodard, Dick, 16, 18
Woodcock dogs, 37, 100
Woodcock guns, 38, 40, 109
Woodcock
    Breeding and wintering grounds, 5, 21, 44
    Colloquial names, xii, 37
    Coloration, 3
    Courtship flight, 7
    Coverts, xii, 144
    Development of chicks, 10
    Edibility, 76, 137
    Flight duration, 49
    Flush variations, 77, 89
    Flying attitude, hen with chicks, 12, 13
    Flying speed, 45, 79, 82, 88
    Flyways of, 44
    Food and drink, 17
    Habits and range, xii, 1, 4, 45
    Incubation of eggs, 9
    Life history, 1
    Migration, xii, 46, 52
    Mortality, 21, 48
    Nesting, 7, 44
    Parasites, 21
    Pesticides, 21, 22, 23
    Physiology, 2, 18
    Recipes for, 137
    Romance of, xi
    Running ability, 101
    Scent of, 102, 103
    Sex and age criteria, 2, 13, 19, 20
    Voice, 6, 28
    Weight, 2
    Whistle of wings, 28
Woolner, Bruce, 98, 160
Woolner, Dick, vii, 106, 124
Wounded birds, 90